Roman Architecture in the Greek World

Edited by Sarah Macready and F. H. Thompson

Occasional Papers (New Series) X

THE SOCIETY OF ANTIQUARIES
OF LONDON

Burlington House, Piccadilly, London W1V 0HS
1987

Distributed by Thames and Hudson Ltd

PRINTED IN GREAT BRITAIN BY
PPC LIMITED,
LEATHERHEAD, SURREY

Contents

Editorial Note

The eighth in the Society's series of one-day research seminars was held on 22nd March 1985 under the title 'Rome in the Greek World: an Archaeological Approach'. It was devoted to a study of the ways in which Roman building design and techniques may have influenced, or been affected by, the architecture of Greece and Asia Minor. The papers presented here comprise most of those given on the day, with the addition of an article on brick construction by Dr Hazel Dodge. On behalf of the Society, we would express our gratitude to all those who contributed to the seminar and this volume, and particularly to Professor Martin Harrison, V.-P.S.A., who chaired the seminar itself, and to Professor Fergus Millar, F.S.A., who has provided an introductory commentary on the theme of the volume.

We have again had to face the problems of the spelling of proper names, rendered rather more acute by the fact that many of these are Greek but in the Roman period. Pragmatism has won: familiar names appear in a Latinized form but others, particularly of buildings, are shown nearer to the Greek.

December 1986

S.M.
F.H.T.

Illustrations

vi

Abbreviations

AA	*Archäologischer Anzeiger (JDAI)*
AJA	*American Journal of Archaeology*
ANRW	H. Temporini and W. Haase (eds.), *Aufstieg und Niedergang der römischen Welt* (Berlin and New York, 1972–)
Aqueducs romains	J.-P. Boucher (ed.), *Journées d'études sur les aqueducs romains, Lyon, 26–8 mai, 1977* (Paris, 1983)
AS	*Anatolian Studies*
AthMitt	*Mitteilungen des Deutschen Archäologischen Instituts. Athenische Abteilung*
AvPerg	*Alterïmer von Pergamon* (Berlin, 1885–)
BAR	British Archaeological Reports
BCH	*Bulletin de Correspondance Hellénique*
BMC	*British Museum Catalogue*
BSA	*The Annual of the British School at Athens*
CIL	*Corpus Inscriptionum Latinarum* (Berlin, 1862–)
FiE	*Forschungen in Ephesos* (Vienna, 1906–)
IG	*Inscriptiones Graecae* (Berlin, 1873–)
IGR	*Inscriptiones Graecae ad Res Romanas Pertinentes* (Paris, 1906–27)
IK	*Inschriften griechischer Städte aus Kleinasien* (Bonn, 1972–)
ILS	H. Dessau (ed.), *Inscriptiones Latinae Selectae* (Berlin, 1892–1916)
JDAI	*Jahrbuch des Deutschen Archäologischen Instituts*
JHS	*Journal of Hellenic Studies*
JÖAI	*Jahreshefte des Österreichischen Archäologischen Instituts in Wien*
JRS	*Journal of Roman Studies*
LIMC	*Lexicon Iconographicum Mythologiae Classicae* (Zurich and Munich, 1981–)
LIWMitt	Leichtweiss-Institut für Wasserbau der Technischen Universität Braunschweig, Mitteilungen
MAMA	*Monumenta Asiae Minoris Antiqua* (Manchester, 1928–)
PBSR	*Papers of the British School at Rome*
PCPS	*Proceedings of the Cambridge Philological Society*
PEQ	*Palestine Exploration Quarterly*
RE	Pauly-Wissowa, *Real-Encyclopädie der classischen Altertumswissenschaft* (Stuttgart, 1894–)
RIB	R. G. Collingwood and R. P. Wright, *The Roman Inscriptions of Britain* (Oxford, 1965)
RömMitt	*Mitteilungen des Deutschen Archäologischen Instituts. Römische Abteilung*

viii

Introduction

Fergus Millar, F.S.A.

THE GREEK WORLD AND ROME

The influence of the Greek world on Rome is a dominant motif from the very moment of the 'foundation' in the eighth century B.C. onwards. The exact nature of Roman influence, or influences, in the Greek world is a much more elusive problem, with many different aspects. They begin with the gradual spread of Roman political and military dominance in the Hellenistic or Republican period; Erich Gruen has recently reinterpreted this process by seeing the evolution of Roman power from the angle of the established inter-state practice of the Hellenistic world;[1] and A. N. Sherwin-White has examined the successive diplomatic and military steps which culminated in Roman control of the Eastern Mediterranean under Augustus.[2] Yet, if we ask how the Greek-speaking world was really affected, first by Roman conquest and then, very significantly, by the Roman civil wars of the forties and thirties, largely fought out in Greek lands, no one has yet gone beyond the powerful and detailed picture drawn in Rostovtzeff's history of the Hellenistic world.[3]

Progress has, of course, been made in various areas. R. Bernhardt has looked in detail at the political and constitutional relations between Rome and the Greek cities in the late Republic;[4] and G. E. M. de Ste Croix's treatment of the class struggle in Antiquity includes an invaluable appendix on the evidence for the partial, episodic, but constant, way in which Roman influence tended to transfer power in Greek cities from popular assemblies into the hands of local élites.[5] This process is certainly relevant to the nature and scale of public building in the Greek cities of the Imperial period, heavily marked by the deployment of private wealth in the form of euergetism, aimed at current popularity and subsequent immortality.

Even towards the later Republic the archaeologically visible traces of Roman presence are still remarkably few. As regards the nature of the coinage in circulation, for instance, the Greek East remained largely separate almost until the reign of Augustus. Then, as Michael Crawford's study of Roman coinage and money in the Republic shows, there is a total and dramatic transformation: the coinage of the entire Mediterranean world is either actually Roman or made up of denominations compatible with Roman ones; and both the Roman and the non-Roman coinage is dominated by symbols relating to the new ruling dynasty.[6]

In the late Republic monuments which either owed their existence to, or were put up in honour of, Roman generals and governors were still comparatively rare.[7] There is little to suggest that a person visiting a typical Greek city in 50 or 40 B.C. would have had the presence of Rome forced on his attention. Here, again, there was then a very sudden transformation, with the spread of provincial and city temples devoted to the worship, in various forms, of the Emperor, or of Rome and Augustus, or of individual members of the dynasty. The theme is treated, as regards Asia Minor, in a major recent work by S. R. F. Price,[8] now supplemented by a very substantial study by E. Hänlein-Schaefer of the temples of the worship of Augustus, from a more strictly architectural viewpoint.[9] In the cases of temples for the Imperial cult, it is a matter of obvious interest to know whether they were or were not distinguished in architectural character, or in sheer size, from other temples, and whether they served as the vehicle for the introduction of the Italian style of temple, on a raised podium and approached from the front, into the Greek world.

Whether we think of city coins representing the Emperor, or of city or provincial temples, or of statues put up in public places to honour emperors, members of their families (male and female), or other prominent Romans, such as governors, we are concerned with products of the communal life of Greek cities, embodying aspects of those cities' reactions to the now established fact of Roman rule. But the theme 'Roman Architecture in the Greek World' might call to mind other possibilities, namely buildings constructed by Rome for governmental and military use. Such a presumption, natural in itself, makes it necessary to emphasize various significant features both of this volume and of the wider subject of which it treats.

Firstly, as the Editorial Note makes clear, the volume is concerned with Greece and Asia Minor, rather than with all the provinces where Greek was spoken and written. So we are not here concerned with Cyrene, Egypt, Arabia, Judaea, Syria, Mesopotamia (made a province in the 190s A.D.), or Thrace or Lower Moesia. Secondly, we are not concerned with those areas of the East where Roman legions were stationed. The Roman military architecture visible in the Roman desert forts of present-day Jordan and Syria is not in question,[10] nor are the Roman military establishments which were carved out of, or imposed on, Syrian cities like Dura-Europus on the Middle Euphrates or Palmyra (the 'camp of Diocletian' constructed in the Tetrarchic period).[11] As regards Roman military construction in all of Asia Minor, nothing could come into the reckoning except (in one sense) roads, and the not very extensive traces of military camps, forts and signal-stations along the Euphrates frontier, extending up to the Black Sea, in the easternmost part of the region.[12]

Most of Asia Minor, in other words, was not a military zone; and equally, in southeast and east Europe, the military zone lay far to the north of Greece, along the Danube. That did not, however, mean that there were no Roman troops at all stationed in Greece, Macedonia and the provinces of western and central Asia Minor. As is well known, the *proconsules* of Achaea, Macedonia, Pontus and Bithynia, and Asia, and the *legati* of Galatia and Lycia–Pamphylia, did each have at their disposal some units of auxiliary troops. The first known discharge-*diploma* issued to an auxiliary soldier serving in the proconsular province of Asia has recently been published.[13] A vivid fictional impression of the brutal impact made by these soldiers on the civilian population of Greece in the second century is provided in Apuleius' novel *The Golden Ass* or *Metamorphoses*.[14]

Even though the numbers of troops under the command of the 'unarmed' governors (Tacitus, *Hist.* ii, 81) of the Greek East seem extraordinarily low, posing a real problem as to how, if at all, the Empire could exert force there, there were some units in each province. Where were they quartered? In converted sections of towns as at Dura or Palmyra? Or in camps? If so, should there not be archaeological traces of such camps? Moreover, we also have to take account of the impact made by civil and military official travellers: governors and officials journeying to, from, or within their provinces; messengers and individual soldiers armed with *diplomata* in a different sense, that is, documents entitling them to requisition transport; and whole bodies of troops, sometimes escorting an emperor, above all on the much-travelled route which led from the Danube through Naissus, Philippopolis and Hadrianopolis to Byzantium, and then diagonally south-east through Asia Minor to the Cilician Gates, Antioch and the Euphrates. A substantial volume of documentation illustrates the tensions created by the demands of these travellers, or travelling units.[15] More particularly, Stephen Mitchell has recently reopened the question of the view put forward by E. Gren, that such military and official movements were actually beneficial, and contributed to the prosperity of the cities, in the Balkans and Asia Minor, on the axis just mentioned.[16]

Two puzzles, which are directly relevant to the possible character of Roman, or Roman-inspired, architecture in the Greek world, arise in this connection. Did such official travel lead to the construction of official stopping-places for the persons or units concerned? If so, what was the architectural character of such establishments, and are they recognizable archaeologically?

A similar problem relates to the Roman governors and their staffs. As is well known, it was normal, even if it cannot strictly be proved for all provinces, that a proconsul should exercise his functions within the framework of a tour which took him round a fixed list of the major towns of his province; in each of these cities he then held judicial hearings.[17] Given such a pattern of activity, it is not self-evidently correct to assume (as is normally done) that one city in each province was recognized as its 'capital'. But, for instance, Apuleius does describe Corinth as the *caput* of the province of Achaea (*Met.* x, 18), and Ulpian records that Antoninus Pius had decreed that, as a matter of precedence, the proconsul of Asia was bound to make his first landfall in the province at Ephesus (*Digest*, i, 16, 4, 5–6). Suppose, then, that we agree that Ephesus was the city in Asia where the proconsul resided unless he were on tour visiting some other city. Where did he live? Was there an official residence, and, if so, was it identical with his primary place of official business? In either case (once again) what architectural character would it have had, and how would we expect to recognize its traces archaeologically? To the best of my knowledge, no building revealed by many decades of excavation at Ephesus has been claimed to be the proconsul's 'office' or 'residence', and it remains wholly unclear what the criteria for such an identification would be.

What these preliminaries amount to is to emphasize that, in looking at 'Roman' architecture in Greece and Asia Minor, we are not looking at the visible remains of any activity or construction by and for the Roman state. Archaeologically speaking, the Roman state remains, in this context, almost invisible. What we are looking at is a much more subtle process of mutual cultural and technical influences. Did any

Roman customs gain a hold in the Greek East in such a way as to require new types of buildings or new architectural forms? Did identifiable Roman building techniques, the use of fired bricks or of load-bearing concrete cores, come into general use? Did the demands of Rome itself, as a major market for architectural techniques and materials, lead to changes of architectural practice in these areas?

In one area, at least, the question of cultural influences is not subtle at all, but quite obvious. That is the introduction into the communal life of the Greek cities of gladiatorial and wild-beast shows (i.e. shows in which gladiators fought either each other or wild beasts, or in which victims were exposed to wild beasts). The evidence for gladiators in the Greek East was collected in a classic study by Louis Robert,[18] whose death in 1985 marks the end of an epoch in the study of the Greek world of the Hellenistic and Roman periods. But though the taste for these forms of show spread widely, and even attracted hostile comment, for instance from Plutarch and Lucian,[19] the evidence for purpose-built amphitheatres is fairly slight (and includes some places, such as Corinth and Berytus, which were Roman *coloniae*); and the archaeological traces of the characteristic oval-shaped amphitheatres as part of the urban landscape of Greek cities are not extensive. Here too, in other words, a very specific medium which might have served for the transmission into the Greek world of Roman architectural styles and techniques does not seem to have done so on the scale that might have been imagined. W. L. MacDonald's important recent study of urbanism in the Imperial period reminds us, however, that temporary sites could have been used, or that in some places, such as Cyrene, a sort of amphitheatre was created out of a theatre by extending the orchestra away from the spectators to form a circular space.[20] As the Martyr-act of Polycarp, set in Smyrna in the mid-second century, illustrates, the stadium of a Greek city could also be used for wild-beast shows.[21]

This martyrdom takes the form of an interrogation conducted by the proconsul of Asia in the stadium, before a large assembled crowd. But by the middle of the second century any notion of a simple opposition, or contrast, between a 'Roman' governor and a 'Greek' crowd would, of course, be long out of date. Immigration from Italy into the Greek world is attested from the second century B.C. onwards. Accompanying that, as is also well known, there came the spread of Roman citizenship to more and more Greeks.

Hence the appearance on thousands of inscriptions and papyri of hybrid Roman–Greek names, predominantly borrowing *praenomen* and *nomen* from the successive Imperial dynasties, while retaining a Greek *cognomen*. Of the twelve ambassadors from Alexandria who presented themselves before Claudius in the few months after his accession in A.D. 41, exactly half already had names reflecting their possession of Roman citizenship: Tiberius Claudius Barbillus, Marcus Iulius Asclepiades, Gaius Iulius Dionysius, Tiberius Claudius Phanias, Tiberius Claudius Archibius, Gaius Iulius Apollonius.[22] One consequence must have followed, with ramifications which it is extremely difficult to discern: the adoption by these families of Roman law. Another ought to have followed, but plainly did not always do so: proficiency in Latin. Individual Latin words and expressions, predominantly official terms, of course entered the spoken and written Greek of the Imperial period.[23] But the extent of a real command of Latin, let alone a true bilingualism, remains very uncertain; it was most probably slight.

A considerable proficiency in Latin must, however, have been required at least of those men from the Greek world who not only enjoyed the Roman citizenship, but entered Imperial service as *equites* or senators. This is not the place to rehearse the evidence for the activity in Imperial service of men from the Greek cities.[24] The representation of the Greek East in the senatorial order in particular has been thoroughly surveyed recently.[25] Two points emphasizing the ambiguity which now attended the relations of 'Roman' and 'Greek' may, however, be stressed. Firstly, the 'Roman' governor or official who appeared before a Greek crowd might himself on many occasions have been a native Greek speaker; and, secondly, while Imperial service might take a man away from home for long periods, or even most of a lifetime, it did not necessarily break his ties with his native city, or mean that he did not perform public roles there, confer benefactions, or pay for buildings.[26] It was only at the end of the third century that the emperors made the fateful concession of allowing a whole range of posts and ranks in the Imperial service to confer a lifelong immunity from city obligations.[27]

By that time, with the emergence of Imperial 'capitals', like Antioch, Nicomedia, and then Constantinople, within the Greek world, the framework of Roman–Greek relations had changed further. But, until then, it would surely be reasonable to see the dual role—local and Imperial—of many leading families in the Greek East as another potential channel through which elements of Roman, or western, taste could have been transmitted. What impression was left by the aqueducts of Rome, the *insulae* of Rome or Ostia, the town houses of the senatorial aristocracy or their villas in Campania? When a senator like Cassius Dio Cocceianus finally went home to Nicaea in Bithynia, in A.D. 229, after an adult lifetime spent largely in Rome or at his villa in Capua, did he bring any ideas about architecture with him?

What we can say for certain is that an interest in Roman history, customs, antiquities and law was a marked feature of the culture of the Romano-Greek upper classes of the Greek cities. Indeed, it would be difficult to exaggerate the extent to which our understanding of 'Rome' depends on representatives of this class and period: Dionysius of Halicarnassus, Plutarch, Arrian, Appian, Cassius Dio.

What has been said here has had the purpose of indicating some aspects of the framework within which various influences from Roman culture may have been felt in the Greek East. It is important to stress that the problem has to be posed in these very indefinite terms. On the one hand, the culture and identity of the Greek East remained fundamentally rooted in the Classical past. On the other hand, the visible presence of Rome, outside those zones where the legions were stationed, was extremely slight. The Empire neither maintained a military garrison in each city nor possessed a bureaucratic hierarchy which controlled the lives of its subjects, nor itself initiated substantial series of public works or public buildings for the use of its employees. The foundation of Roman *coloniae*, at places like Corinth, Philippi, Alexandria Troas, Antioch in Pisidia or Berytus, was another matter; but this was largely a process confined to a single period, the age of Julius Caesar and Augustus. Thereafter genuinely new foundations, involving actual construction, were very rare: Aelia Capitolina, founded under Hadrian on the ruins of Jerusalem, is one notable example.[28] But already in the first century A.D. the creation of *coloniae* had tended to become a matter of the conferment of a title, along with some or all of the rights which might be associated with it. Moreover, this phenomenon itself, as regards Greek sites, is largely confined to the Syrian region: there are very few clear cases in Greece and Asia Minor after the reign of Augustus. Which is perhaps enough to emphasize, once again, that the question of 'Roman' architecture in this part of the Greek world belongs essentially not to the history of government, but to that of culture. It is, in other words, a new and significant aspect of the complex history of the Greek city.[29]

NOTES

[1] E. Gruen, *The Hellenistic World and the Coming of Rome*, i–ii (Berkeley, 1984).

[2] A. N. Sherwin-White, *Roman Foreign Policy in the East, 168 B.C. to A.D. 1* (London, 1984).

[3] M. Rostovtzeff, *Social and Economic History of the Hellenistic World*, i–iii (Oxford, 1941), esp. chs. v–vii.

[4] R. Bernhardt, *Imperium und Eleutheria: die römische Politik gegenüber die freien Städten des griechischen Ostens* (Hamburg, 1971); id., *Polis und römische Herrschaft in der späten Republik, 149–31 v. Chr.* (Berlin, 1985).

[5] G. E. M. de Ste Croix, *The Class Struggle in the Ancient Greek World* (London, 1981), App. iv.

[6] M. Crawford, *Coinage and Money under the Roman Republic: Italy and the Mediterranean Economy* (London, 1985). Note also A. Wallace-Hadrill, 'Image and authority in the coinage of Augustus', *JRS*, lxxvi (1986), 66–87.

[7] See K. Tuchelt, *Frühe Denkmäler Roms in Kleinasien: Beiträge zur archäologischen Überlieferung aus der Zeit der Republik und des Augustus*, i: *Roma und Promagistrate*, Istanbuler Mitteilungen, Beih. xxiii (1979).

[8] S. R. F. Price, *Rituals and Power: the Roman Imperial Cult in Asia Minor* (Cambridge, 1984).

[9] E. Hänlein-Schaefer, *Veneratio Augusti: eine Studie zu den Tempeln des ersten römischen Kaisers* (Rome, 1985).

[10] See esp. D. Kennedy, *Archaeological Explorations on the Roman Frontier in North-East Jordan*, BAR S134 (Oxford, 1985); D. Kennedy and P. Freeman (eds.), *The Defence of the Roman and Byzantine East*, i–ii, BAR S217 (Oxford, 1986).

[11] See R. Fellmann, 'Le "Camp de Dioclétien" et l'architecture militaire du Bas-Empire', *Mélanges P. Collart* (Lausanne, 1976), 173–91.

[12] For this area, still very little explored, see T. B. Mitford, 'Some inscriptions from the Cappadocian *Limes*', *JRS*, lxiv (1974), 160–75, and the admirable survey by J. Wagner, *Die Römer an Euphrat und Tigris*, Antike Welt, Sondernummer (1985); J. Crow, 'A review of the physical remains of the frontier of Cappadocia', in Kennedy and Freeman, *op. cit.* (note 10), 77–91.

[13] B. Overbeck, 'Das erste Militärdiplom aus der Provinz Asia', *Chiron*, xi (1981), 265–76; M. M. Roxan, *Roman Military Diplomas 1978–1984* (London, 1985), no. 100.

[14] See F. Millar, 'The world of the *Golden Ass*', *JRS*, lxxi (1981), 65–75.

[15] See S. Mitchell, 'Requisitioned transport in the Roman Empire: a new inscription from Pisidia', *JRS*, lxxvi (1976), 106–31, for the fullest discussion of the evidence.

[16] See E. Gren, *Kleinasien und der Ostbalkan in der wirtschaftlichen Entwicklung der römischen Kaiserzeit* (Uppsala, 1941), and S. Mitchell, 'The Balkans, Anatolia and Roman armies across Asia Minor', in S. Mitchell (ed.), *Armies and Frontiers in Roman and Byzantine Anatolia*, BAR S156 (Oxford, 1983), 131–50.

[17] The clearest account of this very distinctive pattern of government is given by G. P. Burton, 'Proconsuls, assizes and the administration of justice under the Empire', *JRS*, lxv (1975), 92–106.

[18] L. Robert, *Les Gladiateurs dans l'Orient grec* (Paris, 1940).

[19] Plutarch, *Mor.* 822c; Dio, *Or.* xxxi, 121–2. See Robert, *op. cit.* (note 18), 246.

[20] W. L. MacDonald, *The Architecture of the Roman Empire*, ii: *An Urban Appraisal* (New Haven and London, 1986), 112–14.

[21] M. Musurillo, *The Acts of the Christian Martyrs* (Oxford, 1971), no. 1.

[22] *Greek Papyri in the British Museum*, H. no. 1912; V. Tcherikover and A. Fuks, *Corpus Papyrorum Judaicarum*, ii (Cambridge, Mass., 1960), no. 153.

[23] See e.g. H. J. Mason, *Greek Terms for Roman Institutions: a Lexicon and Analysis* (Toronto, 1974); E. Garcia Domingo, *Latinismos en la koiné (en los documentos epigráficos desde el 212 a. J.C. hasta el 14 d. J.C.* (Burgos, 1979).

[24] See e.g. F. Quass, 'Zur politischen Tätigkeit der munizipalen Aristokratie des griechischen Ostens in der Kaiserzeit', *Historia*, xxxi (1982), 188–213.

[25] See R. Halfmann, *Die Senatoren aus dem östlichen Halfte des Imperium Romanum bis zum Ende des 2. Jahrhunderts n. Chr.* (Göttingen, 1979); S. Panciera (ed.), *Epigrafia e ordine senatorio*, ii (Rome, 1982), esp. 583–683.

[26] See the important paper by W. Eck, 'Die Präsenz senatorischer Familien in den Städten des Imperium Romanum bis zum späten 3. Jahrhundert', in W. Eck, H. Galsterer and H. Wolff (eds.), *Studien zur antiken Sozialgeschichte: Festschrift F. Vittinghoff* (Cologne and Vienna, 1980), 283–322.

[27] F. Millar, 'Empire and City, Augustus to Julian: obligations, excuses and status', *JRS*, lxxiii (1983), 76–96.

[28] See B. Isaac, 'Roman colonies in Judaea: the foundation of Aelia Capitolina', *Talanta*, xii–xiii (1980–1), 51–2.

[29] For which see, of course, the classic work of A. H. M. Jones, *The Greek City from Alexander to Justinian* (Oxford, 1940).

The Impact of Roman Architects and Architecture on Athens: 170 B.C.–A.D. 170

Homer A. Thompson, Hon.F.S.A.

Throughout late Hellenistic and early Imperial times Rome was subject to continuous and pervasive influence from Greece, especially from Athens. The great old monuments, the temples and civic buildings, were standing in Athens in prominent places to be seen, admired and copied by any intelligent visitor. The available writings on architecture, prior at least to Vitruvius, were by Greek authors. As the Hellenistic monarchies declined, enterprising architects in an old city like Athens turned for commissions to Rome. One may recall a rather sour remark by Cicero in a letter to Atticus, then in Athens; the time is 45 B.C.: 'A countryman of yours [i.e. an Athenian]', writes Cicero, 'is enlarging the City [i.e. Rome] which he had not yet seen two years ago, and which he thinks too small to hold him [i.e. the architect] even though in the past it was big enough to hold the master himself [i.e. Caesar]' (*ad Atticum*, xiii.35). One will also have in mind the gentle rebuke which the Emperor Trajan administered to Pliny, his special legate to Bithynia (Pliny, *Epist.*, x.39–40). Pliny had begged for an architect from Rome to help him straighten out some architectural problems in his province. 'You can have no lack of architects', writes Trajan, 'there is no province that does not have experienced and talented people; and do not imagine that it would be quicker to have one sent from Rome, for they usually come from Greece even to us.'

Movement in the other direction, i.e. from west to east, was not continuous but episodic. It was occasioned in most cases by the personal predilections of individuals, usually monarchs or wealthy men. And the impact of such excursions was usually restricted in both place and time. My intention in this paper is to put together, in a roughly chronological sequence, several of the better documented examples of such west-to-east relationships. The net result, I fear, will be of no great consequence for the history of architecture, although several of the incidents may be of interest in themselves.[1]

I

Let us begin with a very familiar example which in various ways is characteristic: I mean the Temple of Olympian Zeus at Athens (pl. I*a*).[2] Lying midway between the Acropolis and the Stadium, the temenos was enormous, about equal in area to the whole Acropolis and its slopes. But the sanctuary seems never to have been very popular in democratic Athens, largely, no doubt, because of its notoriously monarchical associations. The first temple of monumental scale was begun by the family of the tyrant Pisistratus, but was left unfinished at the time of their expulsion in 510 B.C. The Pisistratid builders seem to have laid the foundations throughout, and to have put in place the three steps and some column drums. This was to be the mainland's entry, in the Doric order, in competition with the colossal Ionic temples of the Greek east: Samos, Ephesus, Miletus. The basic plan, an octostyle, dipteral temple with a long cella of characteristically late Archaic proportions, was to be retained through all subsequent periods.

The democracy, when restored at the close of the sixth century, had no appetite for resuming work on the tyrant's project. That was left for another culture-conscious monarch, Antiochus IV Epiphanes, King of Syria 175–164 B.C.[3] While retaining the original plan, Antiochus' architect changed the order from Doric to the now fashionable Corinthian; he appears also to have laid foundations for interior colonnades in the cella, setting them close against the side walls. Most, if not all, of the outside columns with which we are familiar are of the time of Antiochus; but on the king's death the building was left still unfinished and roofless; Vitruvius classified it as octostyle, hypaethral (*de Arch.*, 3.28).

Even in its unfinished state the temple made a great impression on the ancients. Athenaeus (v,p.194a) cites Antiochus' work on the Olympieion as a prime illustration of how that monarch outdid all the other kings in benefactions to the cities and in honours to the gods. For Livy (xli.20.8) the Olympieion was the one shrine that had been begun on a scale worthy of the god. Antiochus was motivated by an Alexander-like urge to spread Hellenic culture and Hellenic religion throughout the world. In his missionary efforts he focused particularly on Olympian Zeus, with whom he did not hesitate to equate himself. In addition to his work in Athens, we are told that he built a temple to that divinity in his own capital, Antioch on the Orontes, and an altar in Jerusalem.

Most interestiing for our present purpose is Antiochus' choice of architect for the temple in Athens. Vitruvius (*de Arch.*, viii, *pref.* 15, 17) tells us his name: Cossutius. Proudly emphasizing his Roman citizenship, Vitruvius includes Cossutius among *nostri antiqui*, but regrets his failure to publish. We can share that regret, for we would gladly know for what reason Cossutius was chosen for such a major commission in Greece. As we have seen, very little new planning was called for, and the design of the capitals followed in the Corinthian tradition of mainland Greece. Perhaps there was no competent Athenian architect available. The great stoas erected in Athens in the first half of the second century B.C. by Eumenes II and Attalus II of Pergamum show such strong Pergamene influence in both design and execution as to suggest that the kings had sent their own architects to Athens. Perhaps Cossutius was outstandingly competent on what we would call the engineering side. The work on the Athenian temple involved some formidable practical problems, not least in the handling of materials. One of the architrave blocks, with a weight of *c.* 23 tons, is one of the largest stones used in construction at Athens in any period. On the other hand, Antiochus' choice may have been based on personal acquaintance with Cossutius during the fourteen years in which the prince had lived in Rome as a hostage. In this connection it may be significant that the rather uncommon name of Cossutius, written in Latin characters, was scratched with the point of a trowel in the still soft mortar of an aqueduct of the second century B.C. at Antioch.[4]

The death of Antiochus in 164 B.C. was followed by another long blank chapter in the history of the Temple of Zeus in Athens. We are told by the Elder Pliny (*NH*, 36.45) that Sulla (presumably after ravaging the city of Athens in 86 B.C.) carried off columns from the Temple of Zeus to be reused in the Temple of Jupiter on the Capitol at Rome. There is no need to question this clear statement; we know from the Mahdia shipwreck that great quantities of Athenian architectural members were shipped westward at this time. But no trace of the Athenian columns has yet been recognized in Rome, nor have scholars been able to detect any certain impact of such imports on the development of the Corinthian style in Rome.[5]

There follows another royal intervention. Suetonius (*Aug.*, 60) reports that a number of friendly kings, being well disposed towards Augustus, 'joined in a plan to contribute the funds for finishing the Temple of Jupiter . . . and to dedicate it to his genius'. We know nothing more of this plan; it may have resulted in some further work on the building, not as yet certainly identified; in any case it did not lead to completion.

That consummation, as we all know, was achieved by the greatest monarch of them all, the Emperor Hadrian. Hadrian was already on intimate terms, so to speak, with Olympian Zeus, as shown, for instance, by their appearance, one on the obverse, the other on the reverse, of a silver medallion struck *c.* A.D. 119–22.[6] Here, in fact, Hadrian, the first Roman emperor to wear a beard, has assimilated his tonsure to that of his Olympian confrère; in doing so he came close also to Pericles. And this is not likely to have happened by chance. As to how much remained to be completed on the temple, we are dependent chiefly on the ancient authors, and they are very laconic. One can be sure of nothing beyond Pausanias' report (i.18.6) that Hadrian dedicated the temple and the gold and ivory cult image of Zeus, 'the workmanship of which, considering its size,' observed Pausanias, 'is good'. We may assume, in view of the material of the statue, that the building was now roofed.

Although Hadrian's architectural contribution to the Olympieion may have been slight, his actual completion of the great building was a very appropriate finale to its long history. The sanctuary became a focal point in the Emperor's effort to bring all the Hellenes together. To quote Pausanias again (i.18.6), 'the place was full of statues, for every city set up a statue of the Emperor'.

In pursuing the story of the Temple of Zeus to its end I have been diverted from my main sequence, which I would now like to resume. Let me say just a word about an incident that occurred in the 80s B.C., a clash between Rome and Athens represented by two powerful personalities: Mithridates VI Eupator of Pontus and Lucius Cornelius Sulla. In the long and bitter struggle waged by Mithridates to free the Greek world of Roman domination, Athens was constrained by old and mutually beneficial ties with Pontus to espouse the cause of Mithridates. This led to the siege of Athens by a Roman army, a siege that culminated on the Calends of March 86 B.C. with a breakthrough in the north-west part of the city. Enraged by the obstinacy and the insolence of the defenders, Sulla permitted a general massacre which he eventually stopped on the intercession of Athenian exiles and Roman senators: 'forgiving a few for the sake of the many, the living for the sake of the dead' (Plutarch, *Sulla*, 14;

Appian, *Mith*. 38). Sulla is reported to have counted himself especially fortunate (*felix*) for having forestalled the destruction of Athens.

The excavation of the Agora and its environs in the past fifty years has shown that buildings as well as bodies suffered heavily in 86 B.C. The Tholos was badly damaged, though it was subsequently rebuilt. Two other substantial buildings along the south side of the Agora, South Stoa II and the South-West Fountain House, were destroyed. Throughout the residential and industrial areas bordering the Agora on all sides the excavators have come on what one might call *Sullaschutt*: masses of burnt debris, choked wells and cisterns. Similar evidence of the sack has been noted by our German colleagues in the Dipylon area. Both in the Dipylon and in the Agora have been found great stone catapult balls in Sullan contexts.

Another notable victim of the clash with Sulla was the Odeion of Pericles, the famous old music hall that nestled alongside the Theatre of Dionysus at the south-east foot of the Acropolis.[8] After the lower city fell to the Romans, a small band of those who were deeply committed to the cause of Mithridates took refuge and held out for a short time on the Acropolis. Before going up they set fire to the Odeion so that the timber in its roofing could not be used by the Romans in their siege operations. All in all, the Roman impact on Athenian architecture in 87/6 B.C. was highly negative.

Regrets were soon to follow. Pompey, visiting Athens a few years later (62 B.C.), contributed 50 talents for reconstruction. Cicero's friend, Titus Pomponius Atticus, who lived in Athens for some twenty years after the Sullan disaster, was repeatedly helpful with financial loans. But for our immediate purpose the most interesting incident of this period is the rebuilding of the Odeion of Pericles. The work was paid for by a king of Cappadocia, Ariobarzanes II Philopator (63/2–52/1 B.C.). In an inscription on a statue base the people of Athens recorded their gratitude to their remote benefactor (*IG*, ii², 3427). In another inscription found in the area (*IG*, ii², 3426) the monarch was honoured by the architects employed by him in the reconstruction. They prove to have been an international team: a pair of Roman brothers, Gaius and Marcus, sons of Stallius, and one Melanippus, surely a Greek. We are told nothing about the circumstances that led to the benefaction, but we do know of friendly previous relations between Rome and the Cappadocian royal family, as well as between that family and Athens. It may be worth noting that the father of Ariobarzanes II bore the epithet Philoromaios, while his mother's name was Athenais. On the other hand, the choice of Roman architects may have been motivated by the experience built up in Rome over the previous century in the roofing of huge temples and basilicas.

About the architecture of the Odeion of Pericles we are embarrassingly ignorant, since the great building has been only partially excavated. This area would be one of the most rewarding in all Athens for further exploration.

Let us return now to the area of the Agora to consider some developments of the Julio–Claudian period (see pl. I*b*, fig. 1). This was a time when many people of consequence were travelling back and forth between Rome and Athens. Even though specific evidence for the movement of architects is lacking, the monuments themselves attest interaction in the field of civic planning and architecture. One must be cautious, however, in considering the direction of movement.

Let us first look at the Market of Caesar and Augustus, the southern of the two great rectangular enclosures thrown up to the east of the classical Agora very much like the Imperial Fora in Rome.[9] Half of the ancient building is still concealed beneath

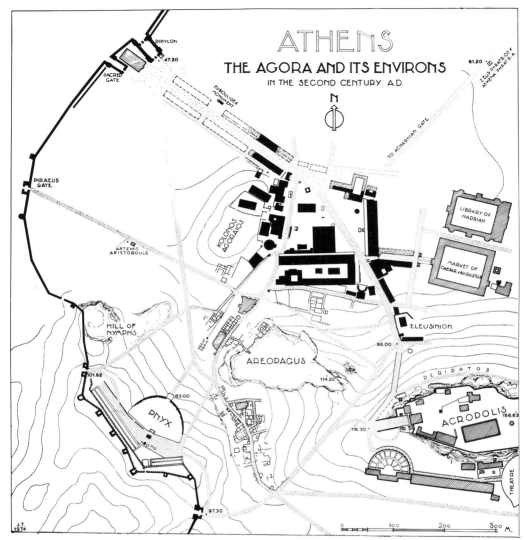

FIG. 1. North-west Athens in the second century A.D. (from Travlos, *op. cit.* (note 2)). Reproduced by courtesy of the American School of Classical Studies at Athens

a mosque and a church, but the main lines of its plan are clear: a marble-paved court bordered on all four sides by colonnades; shops at least on the east side; a fountain house in the south side, a Doric gateway in the west, an Ionic gateway in the east. Conveniently situated to the east are a public clock (the Tower of the Winds) and an elegantly appointed latrine.

A most welcome inscription (*IG*, ii², 3175) on the architrave of the west propylon tells us that money for the construction was given by Julius Caesar and later also by Augustus. Caesar's benefaction is probably to be classed with the contributions noted above by several other distinguished Romans of the time, and to be thought of as motivated in part by a desire to make compensation for the harm inflicted on Athens by the Romans in 86 B.C. Ironically, the outer walls of the new Market Place contain much stonework salvaged from buildings destroyed in the Sullan sack. It is worth recalling that in these same years Caesar is known to have established Roman colonies in both Carthage and Corinth, thus reviving cities that had also suffered from Roman armies.

The Athenian building has been compared with the *kaisareia* known in a number of eastern cities.[10] In the case of Antioch and Alexandria these establishments, as we learn from the literary evidence, were definitely associated with Julius Caesar. Built by him in the years 48–47 B.C., they served primarily as cult places, first for Caesar, subsequently for the Imperial Cult. It is indeed tempting to suppose that the Athenian building, which was closely contemporary, may have been intended to serve a similar purpose. In the present state of our knowledge, however, the evidence favours the view that it was designed primarily as a market place and that it served as such throughout its long life. For the Hadrianic period the evidence is specific: official regulations regarding commerce in oil engraved on the west propylon indicate that this was the principal centre of such trade. Furthermore, the Tower of the Winds, a monumental public timepiece erected about the middle of the first century B.C. and situated conveniently close to the east entrance of the compound, was entirely suited to the needs of a busy market place.[11] It may be taken for granted, however, that here, as in the Imperial Fora in Rome, the great plaza, with its shady colonnades, served also as a centre for social intercourse.[12] The Stoa of Attalus II, erected a century earlier on the east side of the Athenian Agora, with its row of twenty-two shops bordered by a double colonnade on each of its two floors, had also served both commercial and social needs.[13]

The basic architectural scheme of the Market of Caesar and Augustus, *viz.* a large rectangular plaza surrounded by colonnades and entered through one or more propyla, had long been employed in the Greek cities for a variety of purposes. One such building, dating from the early Hellenistic period, had stood at the north-east corner of the Athenian Agora until demolished to make way for the Stoa of Attalus in the second century B.C.; this structure has been tentatively identified as a seat of law courts.[14] In such cities as Miletus and Priene, the closed peristyle, augmented by shops, was used as a commercial market place already in the Hellenistic period.[15] On Delos the large peristyle in the 'Agora of the Italians' (*c.* 100 B.C.) was clearly intended primarily for the social intercourse of the Italians resident on the island.[16]

Although the architectural concept was thus thoroughly Hellenic, the actual construction of the Market Place on such a grand scale in the impoverished city of Athens was made possible only through imperial financing. The result was a splendid addition to the facilities for commercial and social life in the old city. Nor is it impossible that knowledge of what was being planned and slowly executed in Athens had some impact on the similar development that was going on at the same time in Rome, as we shall see below.

The next major building programme in the area of the ancient Agora involved the erection of two major buildings: the Odeion of Agrippa in the south central part of the square and the Temple of Ares in its north-west quarter.[17] The two operations were closely coordinated and were carried out in the years around 15 B.C. The Odeion provided the city with an up-to-date concert hall with a seating capacity of about one thousand to supplement Pericles' venerable, but less convenient, building. The Temple of Ares, on the other hand, was a very fine building of the fifth century B.C.

Salvaged in a semi-ruinous state from its original site in the Attic countryside, it was now moved into the city together with altar, cult and cult image. An inscription (*IG*, ii², 3250) honouring Gaius Caesar, adopted son of Augustus, as 'the new Ares' may be linked with the re-location of the temple. There could be no more striking demonstration of the nostalgic interest in things classical which was so strong in the Augustan period in both Rome and Athens.

The Odeion is an amalgam of typically Greek and Roman elements.[18] The ground plan of the auditorium can be matched among Hellenistic council houses, and the architectural details, capitals, mouldings, etc., are thoroughly Greek. The impressive octostyle Corinthian façade may well have been inspired by the Temple of Olympian Zeus, on which, as we have seen above, some activity was at least planned in the time of Augustus. The idea of lighting the auditorium from the rear through a double row of columns is curiously reminiscent of the Erechtheum. On the other hand, the enormously wide span of the auditorium, *c.* 25 m. with no trace of interior supports, is unparalleled in any known earlier Greek building. In Italy, however, the roofing of such spans can be more than matched, notably in the small 'Roofed Theatre' at Pompeii (*c.* 27·6 m.). Another feature that smacks of Roman practice is the free use of vari-coloured marbles in the flooring of the orchestra and in the stage front. We may suspect that here, as in the case of the restoration of the Odeion of Pericles a generation earlier, a mixed team of Greek and Roman architects was at work. Great builder that he was, Agrippa could well have called on leading professionals both in the capital and the province to join in creating this very remarkable building.

Another striking feature of the Odeion is its placement. The building was set precisely on the north–south axis of the ancient colonnaded square and placed close against its southern closure, i.e. the Middle Stoa. Moreover, the temple-like central mass of the building rose above the lower surroundings like a typical Roman temple above its podium. Thus Agrippa's building, especially as seen by someone approaching on the Panathenaic Way, dominated the whole Agora.

Anyone familiar with Rome will recognize the parallel with a development that had taken place in the Forum Romanum a few years earlier.[19] This was the dedication by Augustus in 29 B.C. of the Temple of the deified Julius Caesar authorized by the triumvirs in 42 B.C. Rising from an exceptionally high podium on the east–west axis of the Forum and pressed close against an older building, the Regia, at the east end of the Forum, this temple was to dominate its setting in much the same way as Agrippa's slightly later building in the Athenian Agora. In view of the personalities involved, one need scarcely doubt a direct relationship. The basic idea could be improved upon at Athens, thanks to a more spacious setting. The Odeion, moreover, with its octostyle façade and Corinthian order, surpassed the hexastyle, Ionic Temple of Caesar in both scale and richness.

The concept of a rectangular colonnaded plaza focused on a temple was familiar, of course, already in Hellenistic sanctuaries.[20] In Rome it first received monumental expression in the earliest of the Imperial Fora, the Forum Julium (fig. 2). Land for the Forum began to be acquired as early as 54 B.C.; work began in 51 B.C.; a temple to Venus Genetrix vowed at Pharsalus in 48 B.C. was added to the programme; forum and temple were dedicated in 46 B.C., in time, that is, to have influenced the choice of site for the Temple of the Deified Caesar in the Forum Romanum.[21] Then followed the Forum Augustum, enclosing the Temple of Mars Ultor vowed by Octavian at the battle of Philippi (42 B.C.) *pro ultione paterna* (Suetonius, *Aug.* 29.2).[22] Temple and

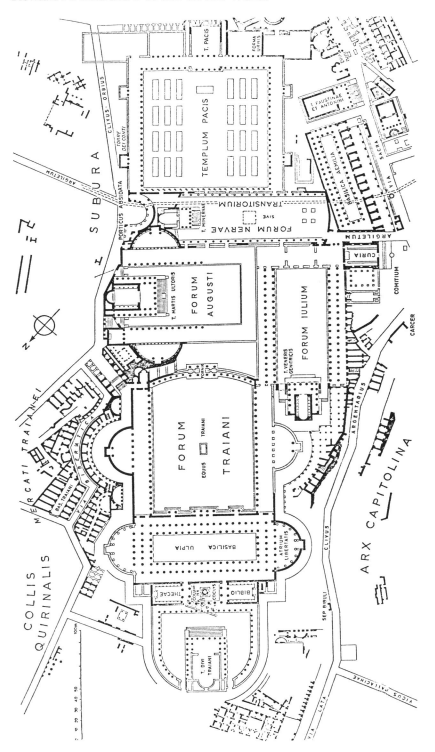

Fig. 2. The Imperial Fora in Rome (from Zanker, *op. cit.* (note 22))

forum were both dedicated in 2 B.C. Because of its history, the plan of this forum is more cohesive than that of Caesar. The façade of its temple, moreover, was octostyle and Corinthian, comparable, that is, with the Odeion of Agrippa.

Since the building programme of the Forum Augustum began earlier but appears to have overlapped the Augustan activity in the Athenian Agora, there can be little doubt of some impact from the side of Rome on Athens. Close contact between the two cities at this juncture is attested by the use of replicas of the Caryatids of the Erechtheum in the sculptural adornment of the Forum Augustum.[23]

Another possible linkage may be considered. As noted above, the construction of the Odeion of Agrippa in the Athenian Agora and the introduction of the Temple of Ares into the Agora were contemporary and closely related operations. One may note, *inter alia*, that whereas the Odeion was set on the north–south axis of the Agora, the Temple was placed on the east–west axis. The altar of Ares, moreover, was placed at the point of intersection of those two axes. The Temple of Mars Ultor in the Forum Augustum, as we have seen above, commemorated the defeat of Brutus and Cassius at Philippi. Is it conceivable that Ares was brought into the Agora as an Athenian equivalent of the Roman Mars Ultor? The Athenians are reported after the assassination of Julius Caesar to have voted for the erection of bronze statues of Brutus and Cassius close to the famous old groups of their own tyrannicides, Harmodius and Aristogiton (Dio Cassius, xlvii.20.4). The location of the older groups has not yet been fixed precisely, but from Pausanias' reference to them (i.8.5), it is clear that they stood not far from where he saw the Temple of Ares.[24]

Roman building activity in Athens, whether sponsored by the administration or by individuals, was heavily concentrated in the Julio–Claudian and Hadrianic periods. This, of course, was the natural consequence of the intense interest among educated Romans of those periods in the culture of classical Greece: its literature, philosophy and visual arts. From the long interval between Augustus and Hadrian we know of only a few minor activities and nothing of great consequence. With the advent of Hadrian, however, the tempo steps up abruptly. In number, variety and quality the building activities carried out in Athens in the Hadrianic period, and for the most part initiated by the emperor himself, bear comparison with the works associated with Pericles in the fifth century B.C. and with Lycurgus in the fourth. The contributions made by various Hellenistic rulers to the ancient city add up to an impressive whole, but no individual contribution by an outsider of any period could match Hadrian's.[25]

Pausanias, in a very unusual passage (i.18.6–9), lists Hadrian's building activities in Athens: the completion of the Temple of Olympian Zeus, a temple of Hera and Panhellenion Zeus, a sanctuary common to all the gods, a building 'in which books are kept' and a gymnasium. To this list may certainly be added a new water supply for the city; perhaps also the large basilica set against the north side of the ancient Agora in the time of Hadrian. A great building of Hadrianic date to the east of the Market of Caesar and Augustus has recently been tentatively identified as the meeting place of the Panhellenion, an organization of Greek states created by Hadrian and based on Athens.[26] Since the annual meetings of the league brought to Athens representatives chosen from among the foremost citizens of many parts of the Greek world, the Panhellenion made Athens an impressive showplace of imperial architecture of the first water.

Hadrian's activities in Athens have been thoroughly discussed in several recent studies, so that little more need be said here.[27] We have already noted the Emperor's completion of the Temple of Olympian Zeus, a splendid gesture in deference to the local architectural tradition. I should like to add only a brief reference to one other item on Pausanias' list, *viz*. a building with 'one hundred columns, walls and colonnades alike of Phrygian marble'. This proves to be an exotic monument, an import from imperial Rome.

This building, which has come to be known as the Library of Hadrian (pl. II) stood to the east of the ancient Agora alongside the Market of Caesar and Augustus, the two of them looking for all the world like the Imperial Fora in Rome.[28] Many people, I am sure, on strolling through what is now a drab part of modern Athens, have been startled to come upon a relic of past grandeur, majestic in scale and dazzling in the richness of its materials. It is hard to believe that what remains is less than half of the façade of a once great rectangular enclosure. Sheltered from the noise of the city was a garden court bordered on all four sides by deep colonnades and overlooked from the east by a row of five rooms. There was but a single entrance through a tetrastyle porch of the Corinthian order set at the middle of the west façade.

In his list of Hadrian's buildings this is the one which Pausanias (i.18.9) labelled as the most splendid. He, too, was struck by the rich materials: a hundred columns of Phrygian marble, a gilded roof and alabaster. But in his day there were also statues and paintings to be seen. Casually, Pausanias adds, 'and books are kept in the building'. It is this remark that has led to the name 'Library of Hadrian'.

There need be no doubt, of course, that part of the building, indeed the largest of the five rooms, was equipped as a library. In the inner face of the back wall one can still see the niches in three storeys that held the book cases. But the neighbouring rooms served other purposes. A few years ago the late John Travlos, engaged in cleaning one of the square corner rooms, detected evidence for a sloping seating floor and a marble-paved orchestra. This was unquestionably a very elegantly fitted-out lecture room; the same was probably true of the other corner room. The purpose served by the smaller intermediate rooms is still to be determined; picture galleries, perhaps. Pausanias' statues are likely to have stood in the colonnades or in the garden overlooking the long pool that ran down its middle.

Clearly we have to do not simply with a library, but with an 'arts centre' of a sophisticated kind and on a scale previously undreamt of in Greece. As has often been observed, and quite rightly I think, the Athenian building is a somewhat improved version of the Templum Pacis in Rome.[29] Begun by Vespasian after the capture of Jerusalem in A.D. 70, and dedicated in A.D. 75, this establishment also combined library, art gallery and garden. It was regarded by Pliny as one of the three most beautiful monuments in Rome (*NH*, xxxvi.102).

In this case I think there need be no question about direct dependence in design on the slightly older building in Rome. An architect in all probability came over from Rome. The next time you happen to be in the Athenian building look closely at what remains of the interior walls: you will find that they are built of concrete faced with triangular bricks in true Roman fashion.

I need say no more about Hadrian's buildings in Athens, for this theme has been very well dealt with in several recent studies. I cannot refrain, however, from emphasizing the number and variety of the expressions of gratitude rendered by the people of Athens to the most generous of all their many foreign benefactors. One example will suffice: a marble cuirassed statue found in the Agora in 1931 (pl. III*a*).[30] This is probably the statue of Hadrian seen by Pausanias (i.3.2) alongside Zeus

PLATE I

a. The Temple of Olympian Zeus in Athens, from the south-west

b. The Athenian Agora from the north-west in the second century A.D. Model in the Agora Museum

Photographs: a–b, Alison Frantz; b reproduced by courtesy of the American School of Classical Studies at Athens

PLATE II

a

b

a–b. Library of Hadrian in Athens. Model in the Museo della Civiltà Romana, Rome
Photographs: Alison Frantz

PLATE III

b. Monument of Philopappus in Athens (c. A.D. 114–16)

Photographs: Alison Frantz, reproduced by courtesy of the American School of Classical Studies at Athens

a. Torso of Hadrian from the Athenian Agora. Agora Museum (S 166)

Eleutherios in front of the Stoa of Zeus. The emperor's cuirass bears the well-known logo: the goddess Athena standing on the back of the wolf of Rome, or, as a cynic might read it, Athens superior to Rome but supported by Rome.

We now leave the Agora and go up to the Acropolis. Standing there *c.* A.D. 150 and looking south-west, Pausanias (i.25.8) saw the newly built tomb of someone whom he called simply 'a Syrian man' (pl. III*b*). The person in question was indeed a Syrian: Caius Julius Antiochus Epiphanes Philopappus, grandson of the last reigning monarch of the little kingdom of Commagene in eastern Anatolia.[31] Philopappus retained the royal title, but he had passed much of his life in Athens, had become an Athenian citizen, an Athenian archon and a friend of Plutarch. But he was also at home in Rome. There he had been appointed *consul suffectus* by Trajan and had been elected to the quaint old club of the Arval Brethren.[32] It was presumably because of substantial benefactions that the people of Athens granted him the very rare privilege of burial within the city walls. There can be little doubt, I think, that arrangements had been made by Philopappus and the design of the tomb worked out by Philopappus himself before his death (*c.* A.D. 114–16). Certainly, the design evokes all three countries with which he had significant associations. Since the monument has been published recently by Diana Kleiner, I may be brief.[33]

The tomb stands on the highest point in Athens outside the Acropolis. The choice of such a prominent location for a tomb is in striking variance with Athenian practice, but one will recall that the royal burial place of Philopappus' family in their homeland of Commagene stood on Nemrud Dagh, the highest point in the kingdom. In strolling around the ruin, one soon realizes that the remaining part was only the gently concave façade of a rectangular tomb chamber entered from the rear. The sarcophagus stood on a platform within a naiskos.

In the main zone of the façade Philopappus is seated semi-nude beneath a vault as though already among the immortal gods. On his right sits Antiochus IV, his paternal grandfather and the last ruling monarch of Commagene; on his left once sat Seleucus Nicator, a distant relative on the mother's side and the founder of the Seleucid dynasty. One recalls the honours paid to his ancestors by Antiochus I on Nemrud Dagh. In the frieze at a lower level Philopappus is driven in his consular procession accompanied by lictors; this scene in Rome marked the high point of his terrestrial career.

The concavity of the façade and the disposition of the sculpture obviously owe something to the *scaenae frons* of the contemporary theatre, while the tripartite articulation of the façade recalls monumental arches, notably that of Titus in Rome. It appears probable, too, that the processional scene on the tomb of Philopappus was based fairly directly on the familiar panel representing the Triumph of Titus on one side of the passageway in Titus' arch. In material and workmanship, however, the tomb sculpture is thoroughly Attic.

In its highly studied composition the Tomb of Philopappus is an interesting product of a multi-national society. Despite its great prominence it seems, however, to have made little or no impact on contemporary practice. There is no other tomb remotely like it in Greece.

Thus far we have dealt with the works of kings and emperors. I should like to close with a brief reference to Herodes Atticus, a private citizen to be sure, but a very remarkable one.[34] Recognized as the leading sophist of his time, a successful teacher, connected with the imperial family through friendship and marriage, Herodes also commanded a fortune which enabled him to compete even with Hadrian in the number and scale of his benefactions in Greece, in Asia, and even in Italy. One may therefore be sure that his staff would have been cognizant of the latest fashions in architecture and of the most up-to-date techniques. In his home city of Athens, with which he maintained a curious love/hate relationship, Herodes carried out two major construction programmes: the rebuilding of the Panathenaic Stadium in marble with a seating capacity of *c.* 50,000 and the building of an odeion seating *c.* 5,000. I should like to look hastily at the Odeion to consider what it holds for our theme.[35]

Herodes, we are told (Pausanias, vii.20.6), intended the Odeion as a memorial to his wife Regilla, who died *c.* A.D. 160. Its purpose was to provide a smaller, more up-to-date theatre to supplement the huge old Theatre of Dionysus. Such pairs of theatres, one open-air and one roofed, are found in a number of cities, notably Corinth and Pompeii. Great skill was shown in the placing of Herodes' new building. By setting it into the south-west slope of the Acropolis the architect avoided the expense of the vast underpinning of masonry usual in theatres of the Roman period. At the same time he availed himself of the magnificent sheltered promenade that was offered by the already existing Stoa of Eumenes—an arrangement reminiscent of the relation between the Odeion of Agrippa and the Middle Stoa in the Agora. In its plan the Odeion of Herodes follows a pattern familiar in contemporary theatres, especially those in the west. Although most of the cavea has been restored for modern performances, the building needs much more study. The existing paper restorations of the *scaenae frons* are unsatisfactory, and, most seriously, no adequate study of the roofing problem has yet been published.

Normally in a theatre of Roman type only the stage was covered, and that by a steeply sloping roof. The Odeion of Herodes, however, is described by Philostratus (*Vit. Soph.*, ii.1.8) as a theatre roofed with cedar-wood, and Suidas also refers to Herodes' building as a roofed theatre (*s.v.* Ἡρώδης· Ἰούλιος). Furthermore, the Greek archaeologist, K. Pittakis, who excavated the building in the 1850s, put much emphasis in his reports on the great masses of burnt debris which he encountered above the ancient floor.[36] The ancient marble seats also show extensive damage from fire. Despite the formidable span (the cavea had a radius of *c.* 38 m.), the evidence favours the restoration of a roof over at least part of the cavea as well as over the stage.[37] While providing shelter against the sun for much of the audience, such a roof would also have facilitated ventilation and lighting.

Although certain problems remain unsolved, it is clear that with the construction of the new odeion Athens possessed one of the best theatre districts of the ancient world, comprising as it did the huge, open-air Theatre of Dionysus, the roofed concert halls of Pericles and Herodes, and the splendid promenade in the Stoa of Eumenes.

By combining the resources of Greece and Rome, Herodes, like the others whose efforts we have reviewed, enhanced the beauty of the ancient city while adding to the amenities of its everyday life.

NOTES

[1] J. M. C. Toynbee, 'Some notes on artists in the Roman world', *Latomus*, viii (1949), 307–16: architecture; ix (1950), 49–65: sculptors; 175–82: painters; 295–302: mosaicists; 389–94: metal-workers, gem-engravers, medallists. A. H. M. Jones, 'The Greeks under the Roman Empire', *Dumbarton Oaks Papers*, xvii (1963), 3–19. G. W. Bowersock, *Augustus and the Greek World* (Oxford, 1965).

[2] J. Travlos, *A Pictorial Dictionary of Ancient Athens* (London, 1971), 402–11.

[3] O. Mørkholm, *Antiochus IV of Syria* (Copenhagen, 1966), ch. 3: 'The relations of Antiochus IV with the Greek world'; G. Downey, *A History of Antioch in Syria from Seleukos to the Arab Conquest* (Princeton, 1961), 95–107; H. von Steuben, 'Seleukidische Kolossaltempel', *Antike Welt*, xii (1981), 3–12.

[4] G. Downey, *Ancient Antioch* (Princeton, 1963), 58.

[5] H. Abramson, 'The Olympieion in Athens and its connections with Rome', *California Studies in Classical Antiquity*, vii (1974), 1–25.

[6] J. P. C. Kent, B. Overbeck and A. U. Stylow, *Die römische Münze* (Munich, 1973), 113, no. 281, Taf. 72.

[7] W. Judeich, *Topographie von Athen*, 2nd edn. (Munich, 1931), 95 f.; *Agora*, xiv (=H. A. Thompson and R. E. Wycherley, *The Athenian Agora*, xiv: *The Agora of Athens* (Princeton, 1972)), 23, index, *s.v.* Sulla.

[8] Judeich, *op. cit.* (note 7), 96 f.; 306–8; Travlos, *op. cit.* (note 2), 387–91.

[9] H. S. Robinson, 'The Tower of the Winds and the Roman Market-Place', *AJA*, xlvii (1943), 291–305; Bowersock, *op. cit.* (note 1), 95; Travlos, *op. cit.* (note 2), 30–6, figs. 38–45; T. Leslie Shear, Jr., 'Athens: from city state to provincial town', *Hesperia*, v (1981), 356–77, at 358–60.

[10] E. Sjöqvist, 'Kaisareion, a study in architectural iconography', *Opuscula Romana*, i (1954), 86–108; J. B. Ward-Perkins, *Roman Imperial Architecture* (Harmondsworth, 1981), 183, 325, 366; Shear, *op. cit.* (note 9), 359 f.

[11] The recent proposal to update the Tower of the Winds to the second century B.C. is unconvincing: J. van Freeden, Οἰκία Κυρρήστου: *Studien zum sogenannten Turm der Winde in Athen* (Rome, 1983), reviewed by H. S. Robinson, *AJA*, lxxxviii (1984), 423–5.

[12] On the cultural role of the Imperial Fora, cf. H. Kyrieleis, 'Bermerkungen zur Vorgeschichte der Kaiserfora', *Hellenismus in Mittelitalien, Kolloquium in Göttingen vom 5. bis 9. Juni 1974*, ed. P. Zanker (Göttingen, 1976), 431–8.

[13] *Agora*, xiv (see note 7), 103–8; Travlos, *op. cit.* (note 2), 506–19.

[14] *Agora*, xiv (see note 7), 60 f.; Travlos, *op. cit.* (note 2), 520 f.

[15] R. E. Wycherley, 'The Ionian Agora', *JHS*, lxii (1942), 21–32; J. J. Coulton, *The Architectural Development of the Greek Stoa* (Oxford, 1976), 62–5, 173 f.

[16] E. Lapalus, *Exploration archéologique de Délos*, xix: *L'Agora des Italiens* (Paris, 1939); P. Bruneau and J. Ducat, *Guide de Delos* (Paris, 1965), 109 f., fig. 18.

[17] *Agora*, xiv (see note 7), 23; Shear, *op. cit.* (note 9), 360–3.

[18] H. A. Thompson, 'The Odeion in the Athenian Agora', *Hesperia*, xix (1950), 31–141; *Agora*, xiv (see note 7), 111–14; G. C. Izenour, *Theater Design* (New York, 1977), 184 f., 264 f.; Ward-Perkins, *op. cit.* (note 10), 25, 265–8.

[19] S. B. Platner and T. Ashby, *A Topographical Dictionary of Ancient Rome* (Oxford, 1929), 286–8; G. Lugli, *Roma antica: il centro monumentale* (Rome, 1946), 198–201; P. Zanker, *Forum Romanum* (Tübingen, 1972), 8–13; Ward-Perkins, *op. cit.* (note 10), 33.

[20] E. Gjerstad, 'Die Ursprungsgeschichte der römischen Kaiserfora', *Opuscula Archaeologica*, iii (1944), 40–72; P. H. von Blanckenhagen, 'The Imperial Fora', *Journal of the Society of Architectural Historians*, xiii (1954), 21–6; H. Kyrieleis, *op. cit.* (note 12); F. Felten, 'Heiligtümer oder Märkte?', *Antike Kunst*, xxvi (1983), 84–105.

[21] Ward-Perkins, *op. cit.* (note 10), ch. 1: 'Augustan Rome'.

[22] E. Nash, *Bildlexikon zur Topographie des antiken Rom* (Tübingen, 1961), 401–10; P. Zanker, *Forum Augustum* (Tübingen, 1968).

[23] E. E. Schmidt, *Antike Plastik*, xiii: *Die Kopien der Erechtheionkoren* (Berlin, 1973), 7–19, Taf. 1–5.

[24] *Agora*, xiv (see note 7), 157–9.

[25] For general accounts of Athens in the time of Hadrian, cf. P. Graindor, *Athènes sous Hadrien* (Cairo, 1934); S. Follet, *Athènes au IIᵉ et au IIIᵉ siècle* (Paris, 1976), 107–35; D. J. Geagan, 'Roman Athens, some aspects of life and culture', *ANRW*, ii.7.1 (Berlin, 1979), 371–437. For Hadrianic building in Athens: A. Kokkou, 'Ἁδριάνεια ἔργα εἰς τὰς Ἀθήνας', Ἀρχ. Δελτίον 25 A (1970), 150–73; Shear, *op. cit.* (note 9), 373–7; A. J. Spawforth and S. Walker, 'The world of the Panhellenion I: Athens and Eleusis', *JRS*, lxxv (1985), 92–100.

[26] Spawforth and Walker, *op. cit.* (note 25), 97 f.

[27] Cf. note 25.

[28] Travlos, *op. cit.* (note 2), 244–52; Kokkou, *op. cit.* (note 25), 162–5; Shear, *op. cit.* (note 9), 375 f.; Spawforth and Walker, *op. cit.* (note 25), 96.

[29] Nash, *op. cit.* (note 22), 439–45, Abb. 536–42; Ward-Perkins, *op. cit.* (note 10), 66 f., 269–71.

[30] E. B. Harrison, *The Athenian Agora*, i: *Portrait Sculpture* (Princeton, 1953), no. 56, pls. 36 f.; *Agora*, xiv (see note 7), 101, pl. 53b.

[31] C. P. Jones, *Plutarch and Rome* (Oxford, 1971), 59.

[32] R. Syme, *Some Arval Brethren* (Oxford, 1980), 113.

[33] M. Santangelo, 'Il monumento di C. Julius Antiochos Philopappos in Atene', *Annuario*, n.s. iii–v (1941–3), 153–253; Travlos, *op. cit.* (note 2), 462–5; D. E. E. Kleiner, *The Monument of Philopappos in Athens* (Rome, 1983).

[34] P. Graindor, *Hérode Atticus et sa famille* (Cairo, 1939); G. W. Bowersock, *Greek Sophists in the Roman Empire* (Oxford, 1969), *passim*; W. Ameling, *Herodes Atticus* (Hildesheim, 1983).

[35] M. Bieber, *History of the Greek and Roman Theater* (Princeton, 1961), 211–13, figs. 712–16; Travlos, *op. cit.* (note 2), 378–86, figs. 492–500.

[36] Ἐφημ. 1858, 1707–14.

[37] W. B. Dinsmoor (*The Architecture of Ancient Greece* (London, 1950), 319) considered the possibility of 'cantilevered trusses and chains, leaving the central portion to be temporarily covered with an awning'. In rejecting Dinsmoor's suggestion, R. Graefe (*Vela Erunt: die Zeltdächer der römischen Theater und ähnlicher Anlagen* (Mainz, 1979), 139, 204 n. 63) confuses the Odeion of Herodes with the Odeion of Pericles. George C. Izenour (*op. cit.* (note 18), 296) rejected the possibility of roofing, and pronounced Herodes' building an unroofed theatre of Roman type, not designed for musical performances. Further study, however, has led Izenour to accept a wooden roof extending over much of the cavea and supported by timber-work like that employed by Trajan's architect, Apollodorus, in his famous bridge over the Danube in which the spans between the stone piers measured as much as 38 m. Professor Izenour has kindly authorized me to report his present views, which will be presented in his forthcoming book on ancient odeia.

Imperial Building in the Eastern Roman Provinces

Stephen Mitchell, F.S.A.

'As I contemplate the greatness of your spirit, it seems entirely appropriate to point out to you construction works that are worthy of your eternal renown and your glory, and which will be as useful as they are splendid.' So Pliny began the letter to Trajan which invited him to support a scheme to build a canal linking lake Sapanca, in the territory of Nicomedia, with the Sea of Marmara. He concluded by remarking that where the kings of Bithynia had failed, the emperor should succeed (*Epist.*, x.41, 1 and 5). Since the days of Gilgamesh, Lord of Uruk, it has always been an indivisible part of a king's role to put up public or sacred buildings for the benefit of his community. More specifically, public building is an activity which stands at the centre of the traditions of munificence and liberality which shaped aristocratic behaviour in the Graeco-Roman world.

The motivation for this form of liberality is rarely made explicit. Public utility was combined with prestige for the benefactor; better still, the permanence of a building might, in the words of a recently published inscription, bring αἰωνία ὑπόμνησις, an everlasting reminder to offset the donor's own mortality. None of this needed to be made explicit, for the whole process of erecting public buildings was not only central to civic beneficence, but imposed a tradition of behaviour and a pattern of expectation from which no public-spirited aristocrat, still less a Roman emperor, could escape, even had he wished to do so.

What follows is an attempt to analyse the pattern of imperially sponsored or funded building, not in Rome, where the subject is a familiar one, but in the provinces, and specifically the eastern provinces of the Roman empire, the principal field in which aristocratic liberality can be observed and documented. This discussion leads on to the borders of an issue which cannot be treated in full, namly the precise role that emperors may have played in the foundation of new cities, or the refoundation of old ones, a topic which has never been fully explored, although it is one where the emperor's role as builder may have been more important than in any other context.

The picture which emerges at the end is one that transcends the rather simple model of aristocratic gift-giving which has been evoked to provide a background to the emperor's actions. The reasons, it appears, lie in the far more intricate and complex patterns that bound the emperor to his subjects, by comparison with those which linked the wealthier and poorer members of a civic community.

Two acknowledgements need to be made at once: in the first place to Ramsay MacMullen's article, 'Roman imperial building in the provinces', published in *Harvard Studies in Classical Philology*, lxiv (1959), 207–35, the only place in the scholarly literature where the theme is treated as a whole; and then, of course, to Fergus Millar's *The Emperor in the Roman World* (1977). Without the conceptual, and indeed the methodological framework provided by that book, it seems very doubtful to me whether the questions which the subject raises could be answered at all.

It is conventional and convenient to draw a distinction between imperial building for military or administrative purposes, and building encouraged or sponsored by emperors within provincial cities of temples, baths, theatres, and the like.[1] The distinction is worth maintaining, and this paper is principally concerned with the second category, but the two are not as separate as they may first appear, and one or two comments on military building seem apposite. For a start, military building clearly involved civilian co-operation and civilian labour, not so often at fortresses and forts (although one may recall the civilian contributions to the repair of Hadrian's Wall, which are not unparalleled elsewhere in the empire[2]), but certainly on the major imperial highways. Pekary, in his excellent book on the roads of the empire, argued that in general the responsibility for road building fell on local civic communities.[3] Not, I would suggest, in straightforward financial terms, for if they, or indeed the Roman authorities, had paid for the roads at anything like the attested levels of cost of road repair, they would have been bankrupt, one and all, in very short order.[4] But rather by providing corvées of labourers, as the provinces of the Ottoman Empire were required to do for Ottoman road building in the late nineteenth century.[5] I suggest that the substantial number of road-building inscriptions which name specific military units as responsible for constructing a road were exceptions to the general rule that civilian labour was pressed into service and used for this purpose.

The emperors were also responsible for the relay posts along the various roads of the empire, but it is significant that this burden, too, could fall on a Greek city, as it did when two citizens of Arneae in Lycia are said to have converted the gymnasium of their home town into a *parochion*, perhaps to accommodate troops involved in Trajan's Parthian campaigns (*IGR*, iii, 639).

Army personnel were also widely used in civilian building, a point well illustrated in MacMullen's study, whose list of examples shows that soldiers were almost as likely to be engaged in building a temple or a bath house as city walls, towers, and gates, with only the proviso that they were more normally involved in large-scale, not small-scale, construction.

Military expertise was highly prized. Witness Pliny's repeated requests for an architect to be sent from Lower Moesia to help his inspection of Bithynian building projects (*Epist.*, x.17b, 39, 41, 61), or Ulpian's later specification that a *praeses* should, where necessary, use *ministeria militaria* to evaluate and assist in the completion of such public works (*Dig.*, i.16.7.1).

Trajan's resistance to Pliny's demands cracked when he was presented with the canal scheme, to be brought to fruition by a combination of military expertise (an *architectus* or a *librator*) and local labour. This was surely standard practice, also envisaged in the recently published Hadrianic letters from Coroneia in Boeotia concerning the draining of Lake Copais,[6] and best exemplified by the famous letter of an *evocatus Augusti* who had been sent to sort out the engineering problems of a badly surveyed aqueduct at Saldae in Numidia (*CIL*, viii, 2728=*ILS*, 5793). But we should note that soldiers were also used to take charge of much more conventional operations, like the *frumentarius* of *Legio I Italica*, who was given citizenship at Delphi in recognition of his scrupulous supervision of the buildings erected there by the emperor Hadrian.[7]

The ambiguity in defining construction as civilian or military is most obvious in the case of building in the cities whose purpose was precisely the security and defence of the empire, namely of city walls. The evidence for wall building under the empire is too diverse to be analysed in full here, but one point may be made, with a single illustration. Collaboration between local civic authorities or individuals and the central administration, in the form of the emperor or the provincial governor, may well have been normal, and it is hard, if not impossible, in many cases, to resolve the problem of where the initiative in these matters originated. For example, an inscription from Odessus in Thrace hails Tiberius as κτίστης τοῦ καινοῦ περιβόλου, builder of the new wall circuit, but honours a local citizen who had paid for a stretch of the curtain and for roofing the wall-walk.[8]

The ambiguity about responsibility is graphically brought home by two inscriptions from Nicaea in Bithynia. One, on the west gate, indicates that the emperor Claudius Gothicus, whose names and titles are given in the nominative, provided walls for the city during the governorship of Velleius Macrinus. The other, on the south gate, indicates that the walls were dedicated to the emperor, the senate and the Roman people, by the city. The former unequivocally suggests direct imperial responsibility and involvement, the latter, seemingly with equal clarity, appears to deny it.[9]

In any given case it is hard to decide what precisely was involved in the imperial patronage and financing of provincial building, and the Nicaea inscriptions raise a serious problem of method in determining answers. Inscriptions often tell us less than we think they do. For instance, the text cut over the original south doorway of the Augustan market building at Lepcis Magna, dating to 8 B.C., simply bears the name and titles of Augustus in the nominative. Taken alone, that would suggest that Augustus himself had been responsible for erecting the building, perhaps especially for paying for it. In fact, another text on the same façade has survived to show that a local citizen, Annobal son of Imilcho, took charge of the construction at his own expense (J.M. Reynolds and J. B. Ward Perkins, *The Inscriptions of Roman Tripolitania* (1952), no. 319). The famous and much discussed letter of the proconsul Vinicius to the people of Cyme in Asia, dating to the 20s B.C., introduces a further twist. Augustus and Agrippa, as consuls in 28 B.C., had ruled that sacred property which had fallen into private hands should be restored to its former sacral ownership. Vinicius, applying the ruling to a particular case which had arisen in Cyme, ordered that when the building had been restored to the god, a new inscription should be carved: *Imp. Caesar deivi filius Augustus restituit*.[10] Yet Augustus' practical involvement in this particular case had been non-existent. Two centuries later, the city of Philadelphia in Lydia asked the emperor Caracalla to be allowed to erect a neocory temple in his honour, naturally at local expense. The emperor's favourable reply was carried on a stone model of the temple, and the architrave carried the text

Ἀντωνεῖνος σ' ἔκτιζε (*IGR*, IV, 1619). The emperor became *ktistes* simply by virtue of having granted the city permission to hold an imperial neocorate.

Nevertheless, we must, presumably, assume that in most cases imperial responsibility for provincial building involved some financial or material commitment on the emperor's part. That said, any and every means of subventing the cities might be adopted.[11] The emperors owned many of the major sources of building materials: mines, forests, brick kilns, and, particularly in the eastern provinces, marble quarries. Thus we find emperors supplying columns for use in Smyrna, at Athens, and at Ostia,[12] paving stone for Alexandria in Egypt and for Syrian Antioch.[13] Direct or indirect financial aid was certainly much more common than the provision of material. The simplest method was for the emperor to remit a city's dues, the taxes or rents that were payable to the imperial treasuries. Tiberius adopted this method, alongside a large cash grant, to help the twelve cities of Asia smitten by an earthquake in A.D. 17 (Tacitus, *Ann.*, ii.47); three centuries later Constantine did the same for the town of Augustodunum in Gaul, to enable it to repair its public buildings and temples (*Panegyrici Minores*, vi (vii), 22.4). The method was simple, requiring the emperor and his agents to do precisely nothing except to desist from tax collection, but there may be a further explanation for the popularity of the method. The imperial liberality which took this form was usually given in response to a petition from the beneficiary. It may have been easier and more tactful for the recipient to ask for a remission of debts, than for an outright cash grant.

Such grants, for all that, were common enough, ranging from the 10,000,000 HS given by Tiberius to the Asian cities, to 65,000 HS laid out by Hadrian for the Lake Copais drainage scheme. The actual transfer of funds could take complicated forms. The best-documented instance concerns the construction of the aqueduct at Alexandria Troas, where Atticus Herodes, the father of the famous sophist, who was then acting as curator of the free cities of Asia, asked Hadrian, on the city's behalf, for three million drachmae to ensure a reliable water supply. The emperor approved, and Atticus Herodes himself took charge of the work until costs reached seven million drachmae, at which point the procurators of Asia wrote to Hadrian to complain that the tribute of five hundred cities was being spent on the water supply of a single one of them. The emperor sympathized with the complaint and reproved his curator, who undertook that he and his son, the famous Herodes Atticus, would foot the bill for anything spent over the original three million (Philostratus, *Vitae Sophistarum*, ii.1, 548ᴋ). One should surely conclude that at least part of the direct taxation, customs dues, imperial rents, or other revenues levied from the province of Asia were simply being diverted to the project. There may be parallels for the procedure in Lycia, where inscriptions from the bath buildings at the cities of Patara and Cadyanda seem to show that Vespasian diverted funds, which had probably been destined for imperial revenues, to local construction projects (*TAM*, ii.1, 396 and 651).

The variety of guises in which imperial involvement and intervention becomes apparent, in these and other cases, is an indication itself of the complexity of the relationship between the emperors and their subject cities. The evidence for imperial building reflects not only the ruler's generosity, but the diverse and numerous ways in which they were seen to take responsibility for provincial affairs.

In 27 B.C. an ambassador from the city of Tralles, which had been devastated by an earthquake, came to Augustus, then in Spain, to ask for aid. Augustus sent a commission of seven senior senators and provided large sums of money, with which

Tralles was rebuilt to take the form which it still exhibited to the sixth-century Byzantine historian Agathias, who tells the story (*Hist.*, ii.17). Precedents for this pattern were well established. When Mithridates VI passed through Phrygian Apamea, in ruins after an earthquake, he gave 100 talents towards its restoration, as Alexander the Great was alleged to have done before him (Strabo, xii.8.18, 578). The same sequence of natural disaster, petition and imperial response recurs throughout the principate. It would be wearisome to go through all the episodes which are on record; the pattern is too familiar to need elaborate comment, but again one point may be extracted for illustration. Private donors regularly, probably in all cases, contributed to the expense alongside the imperial restoration. While the governor of Lycia, Q. Veranius, supervised the building of *Sebasta erga*, imperial buildings, at Cibyra, on the instructions of the emperor Claudius in the mid-40s A.D. (*IGR*, iv, 902), a local citizen, on whom he bestowed Roman citizenship, Q. Veranius Philagrus, provided substantial sums for building on his own account (*IGR*, iv, 914). The earthquake which struck Miletus in the late 40s, and led to Claudian intervention there too, also seems to have been the spur for the well-known liberalities of Cn. Vergilius Capito, who was responsible, it now seems, not only for the baths that bear his name, but also for the *scaena* of the theatre.[14] The Tiberian restoration of Sardis in A.D. 17 was matched by Socrates Pardalas, from a wealthy local family, who restored a temple (*SEG*, xxviii, 928), and the help which Antoninus Pius gave to Stratonicea, Rhodes and the Lycian cities in A.D. 139/40 ran in parallel with the vast benefactions given in the wake of the same earthquake by Opramoas, the millionaire of Rhodiapolis.[15]

Pliny's appeal to Trajan on behalf of his canal scheme had pleaded a combination of splendour and utility to attract the emperor's attention to it. Both qualities traditionally provided opportunities for imperial generosity. Aqueducts were one of the most distinctive architectural features of Roman cities. They were expensive to build, as Hadrian had found at Alexandria Troas, and their construction required highly accurate surveying and sophisticated engineering techniques. Moreover, as Dr Coulton points out (p. 81), they were not a favourite choice for aristocratic display. More than any other type of building, then, they seem to have received imperial subvention. Augustus was responsible, in some sense, for systems at Ephesus and Alexandria, Tiberius at Syrian Nicopolis, Claudius at Sardis, Namasba in Numidia, and perhaps at Ceryneia in Cyprus, Nero at Soli, and Vespasian in various Lycian cities.[16] According to the *Historia Augusta* Hadrian gave his name to innumerable aqueducts. His hand is evident not only at Alexandria Troas, but at Athens, Corinth and Nicaea.[17] At Lepcis Magna he *aquae aeternitati consuluit*, but the money came from a local citizen (J. M. Reynolds and J. B. Ward Perkins, *The Inscriptions of Roman Tripolitania* (1952), no. 358).

But emperors also patronized more decorative forms of building. Augustus did much for the Artemision at Ephesus (*IK*, xi: *Die Inschriften von Ephesos*, i, 19b (Latin text); ii, 459; vi, 1522–4; cf. vii.2, 3501–2, 3513), and rebuilt or restored the Temple of Athena at Ilium (*IK*, iii: *Die Inschriften von Ilion*, no. 84). Domitian restored the Temple of Apollo at Delphi (*CIL*, iii, 14203=*ILS*, 8905), and of course, as we shall see in more detail, Hadrian built the Olympieion and much else besides at Athens. All these were famous buildings in famous centres, but it is interesting to note alongside them some much more modest interventions: Augustus building the stage of the theatre at Iconium in Galatia (*IGR*, iii, 262, 1404), Domitian erecting a portico at Megalopolis, which had been destroyed by fire (*CIL*, iii, 13691), and Trajan carrying out miscellaneous repairs and building work in the sanctuary of Apollo Hylates at Curium in Cyprus (T. B. Mitford, *The Inscriptions of Kourion,* nos. 106, 108–9). The evidence hardly forms a recognizable pattern. The random survival, principally from inscriptions, of information that emperors erected buildings of all kinds in eastern provincial cities, gives us further testimony to the emperor's ubiquitous power, and the benefits which he appeared to bring to his subjects. However, the work which he patronized or funded was not intrinsically different from other types of construction. There was no imperial policy to endow cities with structures which they might not otherwise have had.

The sum total for other imperial building in eastern cities pales into insignificance alongside Hadrian's apparently spontaneous acts of generosity. The historians Dio and the author of the *Historia Augusta* have several remarks to make on the matter,[18] and inscriptions confirm the impression. Cities of Asia by the dozen took their name or titles from him and honoured him as *ktistes*.[19] The aqueducts already mentioned, granaries in Lycia (*CIL*, iii, 6738 (Myra), and 12127 (Patara)), a stoa at Apollonia on the Rhyndacus (*IGR* iv, 121), a shrine at Ionian Metropolis (*IK*, xvii: *Die Inschriften von Ephesos*, vii.1, 3433), the famous Temple of Dionysus at Teos (*SEG*, ii, 588), and perhaps also the great temple at Cyzicus,[20] all received his support. But this, too, amounts to little when compared to his gifts to Athens, above all, and to the other cities of Achaea.

Dio tells us that he built the Olympieion at Athens, and caused the Greeks to build the Panhellenion and to celebrate games there (lxix.16.1–2); Pausanias makes him personally responsible for the Panhellenion (i.18.9). The Olympieion had been begun by Antiochus IV, but at his death in 165 B.C. only the east end had reached the cornice. Sulla carted off some of its columns to Rome, interrupting progress, but Augustus planned to complete it, a task finally left to Hadrian to achieve, between A.D. 124 and 131.[21] Then there was the famous library, with colonnades and stoas, whose chambers had gilded roofs and were adorned with statues and inscriptions, to say nothing of the books, and the gymnasium named after Hadrian, which had been built with 100 columns from his Numidian quarries (Pausanias, i.18.9). The monuments, of course, can still be seen. An arch was built linking the new Olympieion complex with the old Classical city, whose inscription, on the east side overlooking the temple, told the passser-by that this gate led not to the city of Theseus, but to that of Hadrian (*IG*, ii², 5185). Hadrian's treatment of Athens went far beyond that of any other emperor to any other provincial city. Ties of sentiment, religion, and an acute sense of the cultural significance of Athens must have motivated the gifts and provided the rationale for Hadrian's commitment to the place. The Panhellenic movement which he fostered and encouraged required a capital city, and a central focus, which his rebuilt Athens provided.

But it is important to note that his philhellenic endowments did not stop there. We have noted his buildings at Delphi; Corinth received an aqueduct and a bath house, and Hadrian restored the theatre;[22] he rebuilt the temples of Poseidon Hippos at Mantinea (Pausanias, viii.10.2), and of Apollo at Abae in Phocis (Pausanias, viii.35.3). There was a colonnade at Phocian Hyampolis (viii.35.4), and the utilitarian scheme to drain Lake Copais. He made the corniche road from Corinth to Megara wide enough for two waggons to pass one another, and rebuilt the Megarian temple of Apollo in white marble, to replace the existing one of brick (Pausanias, i.42.5).

Achaea, notoriously, had been in decline in the early empire. Hadrian's efforts should surely be seen as a genuine, almost a planned attempt to restore the province to its former glory. Pausanias provides a valuable hint that this interpretation is not anachronistic when he remarks, of Megara, that alone of all the cities in Greece it failed to thrive as a result of Hadrian's efforts on its behalf (i.36.3). If construction work and public buildings are any clear measure of regional prosperity, then Achaea in the second century had much for which to thank him.

This final point raises a crucial issue, too large to be discussed here, namely the actual extent of the role played by emperors not only in founding or refounding cities throughout the empire, but in contributing to the construction which they required. This in turn raises further questions about the intention behind such imperial foundations. Were emperors motivated by the desire to develop the communities and regions where the new cities lay economically? The evidence that I have been able to collect is inadequate to provide a full or clear answer to these questions. If any generalizations are possible, I suspect that they will take a negative form: the pattern of imperial city foundations is blurred and indistinct, not conforming to any well-defined model of behaviour.

A subject that at first sight might seem easy to investigate, a simple matter of emperors paying for the erection of public buildings, following a well-ordered and predictable pattern of aristocratic liberality, proves in the event to be far more complicated. The model by which we should interpret imperial generosity and largesse must correspond to the vastly more complex role that emperors played in the lives of their subjects. At a simple level, the military and administrative requirements of governing an empire, and the structures and institutions to which they gave rise, led to building programmes which inevitably encroached on the world of the subject cities. These might contribute labour or funds for military building, or might themselves benefit from military expertise and muscle-power in their own civic building projects. Aside from this, the patterns of imperial patronage of strictly civic schemes were dictated by other aspects of the emperor's position in the Roman world. His ownership of important sources of raw materials enabled him to support building projects in the most basic way; his control of revenue raising made it possible for him to subsidize construction simply by offering tax exemption; his actual wealth gave him opportunities for direct financial patronage on a scale that dwarfed private undertakings. The dynamics and pattern of imperial administration, according to which the emperor tended to adopt the passive role of responding to requests and petitions from his subjects, profoundly affected the nature of imperial building; aid was frequently granted in response to appeals after earthquakes or other natural disasters. On the other hand, ties of religious or cultural sentiment, or personal attachment to a particular place, lay behind acts of spontaneous generosity, which must still explain a sizeable number of cases where emperors paid for construction in eastern cities, and above all underlie the behaviour of Hadrian towards Athens and Achaea. We perhaps know least about an area of imperial building which may have been more important than any other, the actual contributions made to the newly founded cities which sprinkle the map of the eastern Roman empire.

Military administration, taxation, imperial ownership of land and raw materials, the administrative pattern of petition and response, and the foundation of new cities, are some of the dominant themes of imperial history, which helped to create the kaleidoscopic pattern of relationships which bound the emperor to his subjects.

Imperial building and construction has to be considered in relation to all of them. It is scarcely a matter of surprise, then, that the motives, modes and results of the emperor's activities as builders should appear so diverse and various.

NOTES

[1] Cf. L. Robert, *Études anatoliennes* (Paris, 1938), 89 n. 2.

[2] *RIB*, nos. 1672–3, 1843, 1962, 2022; see also MacMullen, *op. cit.* (p. 19 above), 220–1 with notes.

[3] T. Pekary, *Untersuchungen zu den römischen Reichsstrassen* (Bonn, 1968). See, too, the remarks of J. and L. Robert, *Fouilles d'Amyzon* (Paris, 1983), 30–2.

[4] The relevant inscriptions are cited and discussed by Pekary, *op. cit.* (note 3), 93–5.

[5] For Ottoman road building, see V. Cuinet, *La Turquie d'Asie* (Paris, 1892), i, 271; iv, 27.

[6] See Robert, *op. cit.* (note 1), 85; J. M. Fossey, *ANRW*, ii.7.1 (1979), 568 ff.; *SEG*, xxxii, 460–3.

[7] Robert, *op. cit.* (note 1), 88–9.

[8] *Inscriptiones Graecae in Bulgaria Repertae*, i² (Sophia, 1970), no. 57.

[9] *IGR*, iii, 39 and 40; S. Şahin, *IK*, ix: *Katalog der antiken Inschriften des Museums von Iznik (Nikaia)*, i (Bonn, 1979), nos. 11 and 12.

[10] R. K. Sherk, *Roman Documents from the Greek East* (Baltimore, 1969), no. 61.

[11] As MacMullen pointed out, *op. cit.* (p. 19), 210.

[12] *IGR*, iv, 1431; Pausanias, i.18.9.; *Scriptores Historiae Augustae, Tacitus*, 10.5.

[13] *IGR*, i, 1138; Malalas, *Chron.*, 280, 20 ff.

[14] For Claudian subventions after this earthquake, see C. Habicht, *Göttingische gelehrte Anzeiger* (1960), 163. For Vergilius Capito's buildings, see A. von Gerkan and P. Krischen, *Milet*, i.9 (Berlin, 1928), 23–49. The inscription from the *scaena* of the theatre is to be published by P. Herrmann and D. McCabe in a forthcoming number of *Istanbuler Mitteilungen*.

[15] The sources are collected by D. Magie, *Roman Rule in Asia Minor* (Princeton, 1950), i, 631–2; ii, 1491–2 n. 6; and by L. Robert, *BCH*, cii (1978), 401–2.

[16] Augustus: *IK*, xii: *Die Inschriften von Ephesos*, ii (Bonn, 1979), nos. 401–2; *ILS*, 975; Tiberius: *CIL*, iii, 6703; Claudius: *CIL*, iii, 409; *CIL*, viii, 4440 = *ILS*, 5793; T. B. Mitford, *Opuscula Atheniensia*, vi (1950), 17 no. 9; Nero: Mitford, *op. cit.*, 28 no. 15; Vespasian: *TAM*, ii.1, 396, 651; J. J. Coulton, *PCPS*, xxix (1983), 9 with n. 28.

[17] *Scriptores Historiae Augustae, Hadrianus*, 20, 5; *CIL*, iii, 549; Pausanias, ii.3.5; viii.22.3; Şahin, *op. cit.* (note 9), i, no. 55.

[18] Dio, lxix.5.2–3; 10.1; *Scriptores Historiae Augustae, Hadrianus*, 12, 2; 13, 6; 19, 1; 20, 5.

[19] M. Le Glay, *BCH*, c (1976), 357–64.

[20] For a summary of the evidence and problems concerning this building, see S. R. F. Price, *Rituals and Power. The Roman Imperial Cult in Asia Minor* (Cambridge, 1984), 251.

[21] The evidence is summarized in J. Travlos, *A Pictorial Dictionary of Ancient Athens* (London, 1969), 402–11.

[22] Pausanias, ii.3.5; viii.2.3; R. Stillwell, *Corinth*, ii: *The Theatre* (Princeton, 1952), 136–40.

The Refounding of Corinth: some Roman Religious Attitudes

C. K. Williams, II

Upon entering the gates of Corinth in 146 B.C., Mummius sold the Corinthian women and children into slavery and killed its male population, putting an end to what had been one of the largest and wealthiest cities of Greece for over 500 years. He dismantled crucial parts of the fortification system, looted the city of its art and valuable properties and left the city an unpopulated ruin. For 102 years Corinth remained a ruin, probably with squatters, but without a political life.[1] During this interval the land that previously formed the *politeia* of Corinth was the *ager publicus* of Rome, with its use determined by leasing in Rome itself.

Since the Romanization of the Corinthia is indeed a broad subject, I would like to limit the present study to the religious attitudes and buildings of Laus Julia Corinthiensis. Thus, one might look first at the forum of this new city (figs. 3 and 4).[2] The scale of all the temples around the newly laid-out forum is exceedingly small as compared to the vastness of the open space. Even the arrangement of the structures themselves is not especially Roman, although the design and architectural detailing of the first- and second-century temples at the west end of the forum are definitely Italic, not Greek; note the podium-prostyle form (fig. 5) and the construction techniques, especially the poros-revetted concrete cores.[3] Architectural elements, such as the Tuscan order, speak for themselves. In fact the Tuscan order appears to have been quite popular in Corinth. In particular, the design of the temples at the west end of the forum, which were dedicated to major gods and goddesses such as Venus and Apollo, is even more Roman, I think, than the original publication would lead one to suspect. For example, the podium of Temple G, as now preserved, shows no evidence for an associated staircase on its façade.[4] But being built in the Roman architectural tradition, the steps would have been a separate element added to the podium, just as in Italy one finds temples with added flights of steps, the principle illustrated vividly in

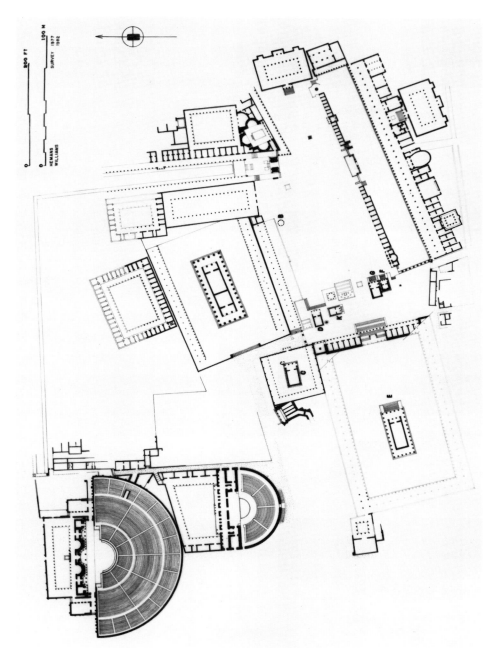

FIG. 3. Plan of central Corinth at the time of Pausanias, later second century A.D.

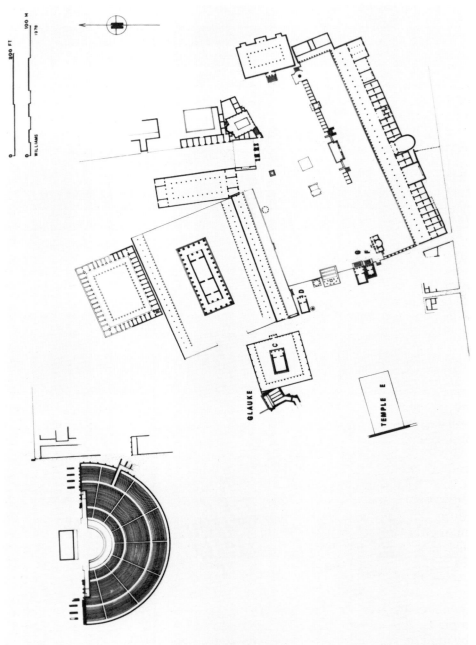

FIG. 4. Plan of Corinth, before A.D. 77

the Temple of Faustina in Rome. As in the Faustina temple, many examples also carry their temple altar low on the staircase. Scranton mentions no altar foundations for any of the temples of the west end of the Corinthian forum except in front of his podiumless Temple of Dionysus.[5] I suggest that in each of the Corinthian podium temples the altar would have been built upon those missing steps. To summarize, then, the main visual difference between the Corinthian temples and those erected in Rome, Ostia, or in the new North African colonies is in their scale, with the Corinthian temples being much smaller in relation to the open forum than were their Italian counterparts.

An addition to the Corinthian forum can be distinguished in Temple E immediately west of the forum; the complex as published is a colonnaded rectangle in the midst of which stands the so-called Temple of Octavia. The initial temple was constructed on the site before A.D. 38/39 in a slightly smaller form than its replacement of the last quarter of the first century.[6] Although not recognized in the original publication, clear evidence shows that the first Roman temple was backed up against its west temenos wall. This arrangement suggests parallels with the Forum of Augustus in Rome, which, like this Corinthian example, was a unit added to an original city-centre. The interesting fact is, however, that, when Temple E and its enclosing colonnade were rebuilt, the temple was placed free-standing within its court, rather than being built against the back side of the court as in the original design. Note, also, how much more space was left between the flanks of the second-phase Temple E and its side stoas as compared with the arrangement in the Imperial Fora at Rome. Even though the design of the Corinthian temenos became more Greek during its rebuilding, the Roman podium was introduced only for the temple in its second phase.

At this point one fact should be noted. If a logical interpretation of the text of Pausanias is followed here, Temple E should definitely be identified as the Temple of Octavia, which he mentions.[7] If this temple housed an Olympian god, he neglected to tell us of its function. Certainly the safest assumption is that Temple E was built to house the Imperial Cult. But in accepting the identification and argument, one must then consider certain implications. A quick comparison shows a distinct difference in size and grandeur between the large Temple E and the relatively insignificant temples at the west end of the forum. One is tempted to see in this evidence that the emphasis in official religion turned from the Olympian gods in the course of the first century A.D. towards the Imperial Cult. The ultimate statement of this attitude occurs during the rule of Commodus when the early Roman Fountain of Poseidon was dismantled and a temple in honour of Commodus was erected over its ruins at the west end of the forum (fig. 5). The site selected is ideal, a focus at the centre of the row of Olympian temples at the west end of the forum, and all achieved at minimum cost with maximum effect.[8]

I suggest that emperor worship was introduced early, probably related to the establishment of the Caesarea contests at Isthmia. A Corinthian coin struck within the reign of Augustus suggests that a temple existed at Isthmia or in Corinth with an epistyle inscribed with 'CAESAR'. One can say with certainty, however, that the cult had taken root in Corinth at least by the time of Caligula, attested then by the erection of Temple E. According to the initial publication, the construction of Temple E is fixed by numismatic evidence to after A.D. 38/39. I suggest that the temple was built under Tiberius or, possibly, earlier.[9] Whichever date one chooses, the date is close to, and possibly related to, the addition of the Imperial Games (Sebastea) to the already

FIG. 5. East elevation of Temple H (Temple of Commodus) at Corinth
Drawn by J. Buckley

established Caesarea and Isthmian games over which Corinth presided.[10] By the beginning of the Flavian period the Imperial Cult had grown to such proportions that Temple E could be reconstructed within a magnificent court at the centre of the city, following the phenomenon at Rome, where imperial forum after imperial forum was being added to the original Forum Romanum. This certainly suggests the escalation of the Imperial Cult in Corinth from the time of Tiberius onwards.

In illustrating how Roman the Corinthian settlers were in their religious attitudes, as compared with their Greek neighbours, one might cite a special example to make the point clearer. Her status as a Roman colony rather than a Greek city appears to have coloured Corinth's thinking. This can be seen, for example, by comparing her with Athens in the same period. No evidence among the inscriptions and sculpture exists for a Corinthian cult of Roma before the Hadrianic period, and even the one Corinthian example of the Hadrianic period that does exist may be simply a sculptural monument erected along the Lechaion Road devoid of cult significance. This monument now exists only as a rusticated throne inscribed with the names of the hills of

Rome.[11] But the cult of Roma is attested in Athens as early as the third century B.C., with an additional cult of Roma instituted on her acropolis in an effort to ingratiate herself with Rome after Actium. Athens had upset the reigning monarch, Augustus, through her hospitality to enemies of the Roman State, including Mark Antony; thus she felt it advantageous to establish the cult of Roma and Augustus, probably east of the Parthenon.[12] This cult of Roma was a totally political device whereby a non-Roman population could celebrate and flatter the Roman people.[13] Corinth, where support of Mark Antony was at least as strong as in Athens, apparently did not adopt this sycophantic posture. Failure to do so would not have been illogical, because the Corinthians were already citizens of Rome, or wished to be. Since they felt themselves to be Roman, it would have been meaningless for them to establish the cult; at this stage it might well have appeared as though they were establishing a cult to themselves, i.e. the populus Romanus. It was only when the Spanish provincial emperor, Hadrian, established the cult of Roma and Venus in Rome and the concept of the cult changed to that of Roma as the personification of the Romanized world order that a cult of Roma would be appropriate in Corinth. The fact that she was used as a symbolic or didactic figure in the pediment of Temple E well before the Hadrianic period does not invalidate the argument.

From the above discussion, I think it is clear that the Romans were not trying to coat their new religious facilities in the colony with any spirit of Hellenism, at least not when trying to establish cult areas. But what did the Romans do when they re-established a pre-Roman Corinthian cult on the same ground that it had occupied before the city was destroyed in 146 B.C.? There is literary evidence that some Greek cult ritual, although known to the Romans, was not reinstated by the new Roman colonists, even though the cult or cult monuments were re-established. For example, Pausanias tells us, when referring to Medea and her children, that 'after Corinth was laid waste by the Romans and the old Corinthians were wiped out, the new settlers broke with the custom of offering those sacrifices to the sons of Medea, nor do their children cut their hair for them or wear black clothes'.[14]

Archaeologically, this attitude of editing for contemporaneity, although surprising when considering the conservative nature of the Romans in matters religious, is borne out in a number of places. The Temple of Apollo, securely seated on a limestone ridge overlooking the centre of the city, was redesigned in the Roman style. Apparently the colonists were determined to reshape the Corinthian landscape more to their liking. No apparent sympathy was shown for preservation of the Greek temple plan or of the operation of the cult as known in the Greek period. The entrance of the temenos at the south-east angle of the hill was abandoned for a Roman axial entrance at the west end. The east end of the ridge was the place where, probably, the original altar of the cult had stood, but the ridge was cut away in the search for convenient building material as the Romans reconstructed their new city out of the Greek ruins. The east end of the ridge, with its temenos, was truncated by quarrying, and a large basilica was erected. Apparently, too, the Archaic plan of the interior of the temple itself was unsatisfactory to the Roman colonists, for they removed its interior columns. The cella columns thus removed were re-erected at the south-west corner of the forum as a free-standing colonnade extending northward from the South Stoa to define the Roman forum at this point. As a result of this work, the plan of the Temple of Apollo was changed from a secos composed of two colonnaded rooms, into, most probably, a single large column-free room. This alteration was not made because the original interior columns were in poor shape after the hundred years of abandonment, for they were reused, as stated above, by the Romans in their colonnade at the west end of the South Stoa.

Robinson, the most recent excavator of Temple Hill, has presented the theory that the temple itself was not only rebuilt, but that its eastern entrance through the pronaos was abandoned for one at the west, on the axis of the new Roman entrance to the temenos from the road to Sikyon.[15]

It is possible to see the same principles in operation in another of the city's cults, that of the Armed Aphrodite whose temple crowned Akrokorinthos. An official state cult had been established to celebrate this goddess from early in the life of the Greek city. In fact the presence of Protogeometric and Geometric pottery might even suggest that the cult of a protecting goddess goes back on this site to the earliest Dorian phase of the city. Herodotus records that the goddess had been prayed to to preserve the Corinthians from the Persians during the Persian War, at the time when the Peloponnesians had dropped back to a defence line at the Isthmus. After that crisis was successfully resolved, a bronze tablet was set up recording the prayer service offered in their time of need by the priestess and the *hierodouloi* of the cult. Now no architectural remains are to be found which can be associated with that cult in any of its Greek phases except cuttings in bedrock at the summit of the acropolis. For the Roman period, however, we have Corinthian coins that show the temple of Aphrodite as restored on Akrokorinthos (pl. IV*a–b*). As one might expect, the temple is prostyle on a high podium, with a flight of steps only at the east, indicating that the temple was not altered, but totally rebuilt, by the Romans.

I am on weaker ground when talking about the Greek and Roman cult statues of this sanctuary, but I think that as radical a change was made with the image as with the temple itelf, once the Romans re-established Aphrodite in her city. Although our knowledge about the cult statue of the sanctuary and the iconography of its cult is now well edited by the passage of time, we do know that the cult was, originally, focused around an armed goddess who was protectress of the city, served by *hierodouloi*. By the time that we have iconographic evidence of her cult, that evidence is Roman (although some are inclined to suggest that the evidence may be partly Hellenistic).[16] In any case the evidence from Roman coins shows the cult statue of Aphrodite holding a shield, but using it as a mirror to reflect her beauty in its polished surface (pl. IV*b–c*; see also lamp, pl. IV*d*).[17] From parallels in Roman wall paintings, one can take the interpretation one step farther: it is not the shield that an Armed Aphrodite would have carried, but one borrowed from Ares. With Roman Corinth no longer an independent state and no longer in need of a guardian goddess for her now non-existent walls, what use did the city have for a goddess of war and protection? Instead, it was her function as a goddess of love that satisfied the requirements of the new colonists (pl. IV*e–g*). Tyche, wearing her mural crown, was given a temenos among the temples of the west end of the Roman forum. She took on all responsibility for the political and economic well-being of Corinth.

In summary then, the evidence, I think, suggests that the Romans knew about and tried to revive the Greek sanctuaries of the city, if possible even on their original sites, but were not concerned to restore them to their original form or recreate their original Greek ritual with any great precision or accuracy. Roman 'modernization' seems to have been much preferred to ancient Greek authenticity.

The Asklepieion of Corinth, however, when repaired by the Romans, was

PLATE IV

a   *b*   *c*

a. Coin 25–43. Tetrastyle prostyle Temple of Aphrodite on Akrokorinthos. Domitian ($\frac{1}{1}$)

b. Coin Agora SE, June 4, 34. Tetrastyle temple with its two central columns removed to show cult statue of Aphrodite with shield, on Akrokorinthos. Marcus Aurelius ($\frac{1}{1}$)

c. Coin T-26-211A. Aphrodite with shield, Eros at right. Cult statue on coin of Corinthian anon. series. Hadrian ($\frac{1}{1}$)

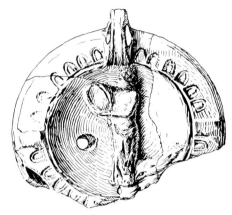

d. Corinthian Roman lamp showing Aphrodite with shield, a representation of the cult statue on Akrokorinthos. L-214 ($\frac{2}{3}$)

e. Marble statuette of Roman cult statue on Akrokorinthos. S-2548 ($\frac{1}{4}$)

f. MF-1985-25

g. MF-1985-12

f–g Terracotta figurines: Aphrodite adapted to Roman tastes and with Flavian hairstyles ($\frac{1}{4}$)

The Roman cult of Aphrodite on Akrokorinthos

apparently restored very much along the original Greek lines, at least as far as its court and temple were concerned, although the ramp to the lower court, the fountain associated with it, and, apparently, the dining rooms of the original cult were obliterated. Restoration of the temple was undertaken in the very early years of the Roman colony, dated by a painted inscription on the epistyle of the temple to around 25 B.C.[18] The temple must have been in relatively good condition at the time that the reconditioning was carried out and, as a result, the colonists accepted the solution of repairing an already existing temple according to the original Greek design rather than re-erecting it as a podium-style Roman temple. Thus, in this case we have a Greek remain restored to its original form, but, most likely, only for the sake of expediency.

And what about the Fountain House of Glauke, a building that is so carefully carried out in the Greek style that, until recently, it was considered by scholars to be an honoured remain of the pre-Roman city? It lies about 60 m. north-west of the forum, cut out of the bedrock of what, until Roman times, had been a limestone ridge. This ridge ran westward from the Lechaion Road valley and at its eastern end supported the sanctuary of Apollo. By eliminating most of the ridge west of the sanctuary the Temple of Apollo was made to appear as though it occupied the highest part of a hill, rather than the lower, east, end of a long ridge. Within the quarry itelf only one block of stone was left *in situ*; this was fashioned into the Fountain House of Glauke. The Greekness of its design can be seen most clearly when it is compared to the Spring House of Peirene or the Fountain House in the upper town of Perachora, a Corinthian town on the north side of the Gulf of Corinth.[19] The Fountain House of Glauke is composed of four, long, parallel reservoirs cut into living rock with a deep, narrow drawbasin, divided into three parts and running at right-angles across their short end. In front of the drawbasin, that is, along the other long side of the three-part basin, is a covered porch from which people could draw what water they wanted. The design that the Greek Corinthians had developed was quite different from that of a Roman nymphaeum or public fountain such as that of Poseidon at the west end of the forum. A number of details suggest, however, that here a Roman design may deliberately have masqueraded as a Greek one. The facts which support this are, first, that the Fountain House of Glauke never had a natural source of water, as do all the other early Greek fountains of this form. That one of the fountains famous in early Corinthian mythology was carved totally from bedrock, yet had its water piped in from a distance, seems suspect. Add to that some of its construction techniques: the stone quarried from within the reservoirs appears to have been removed through the front façade of the fountain house or, rather, through a cut made under the front façade. This passageway allowed stone to be dragged on to the floor of the Roman quarry that surrounds Glauke. Although it cut through the drawbasin it appears to be contemporary with the construction of the fountain house and with the Roman quarrying operation. Thirdly, the porch of the Fountain House of Glauke, although cut out of bedrock, is fashioned in the shape of a barrel-vaulted roof. A Classical Greek would have imitated slabs or coffering here; the earliest use of a vault to roof a public space at Corinth should certainly not be expected before the Macedonian period, if then. But not only that, the vault used for the porch of Glauke is wide and flattened, not semicircular as would be expected if it were imitating Hellenistic vaulting. Here we have one telling element of Roman design within an otherwise totally Greek programme.

With Glauke we have, then, an example of deliberate architectural eclecticism within Laus Julia Corinthiensis. I assume that cult buildings, such as temples, were considered better if they were in the Roman style unless it was viable to repair a Greek ruin more cheaply. With the Fountain of Glauke we see a different attitude. The Romans, I assume, eliminated the original Fountain House of Glauke in their quarrying operation west of the Temple of Apollo, perhaps because it did not fit into their urban street plan or because its Greek site had to be used for some more important monument. The fountain house was then located within the quarry, where it could be used by travellers on the road to Sikyon or for persons in the odeion, who only had to walk across the street at intermission to refresh themselves. But why did they not build a modern nymphaeum? I would suggest that the design was determined by the literary spirit of the educated Roman colonist, who wanted to be able to show a monument of ancient Corinth fitting, as he saw it, the myth of Medea as it was passed down, even into the time of Pausanias (ii.i.6), perhaps justifying the local version of the tragedy over that set down by Euripides (*Medea*, 1125–1226).

In conclusion, however, may I just note that the Roman attitudes of Julius Caesar's colony did not emerge intact from exposure to the Greek influences and pressures that culminated in the Hadrianic wave of Pan-Hellenism.[20] Thus, it is not mere rhetoric when, in the early second century, Dio Chrysostom observes to the Corinthians that: 'you have become thoroughly hellenized, even as your own city has'.[21]

NOTES

[1] For evidence of squatters, see C. K. Williams, II, 'Corinth 1977, Forum Southwest', *Hesperia*, xlvii (1978), 21–3; C. K. Williams, II, and P. Russell, 'Corinth: excavations of 1980', *Hesperia*, l (1981), 27, 34–44.

[2] R. L. Scranton, *Corinth*, i.3: *Monuments of the Lower Agora and North of the Archaic Temple* (Princeton, 1951). This is the main publication of the Roman temples of the forum.

[3] *Ibid.*, 10 (Hermes); 37 ('Heracles' and Poseidon); 52–3 (Pantheon).

[4] *Ibid.*, 53.

[5] For the altar in front of the Dionysion, see, *ibid.*, 91, figs. 48–9.

[6] R. Stillwell, R. L. Scranton and S. E. Freeman, *Corinth*, i.2: *Architecture* (Cambridge, Mass., 1941), 166–84. The construction date for Temple E is given by Freeman in that publication (p. 178) as Caligulan; the evidence is a Corinthian coin bearing the name of the duovir P. Vipsanius Agrippa. The duovir is now dated by Kent to A.D. 39–40, early in Caligula's reign: J. H. Kent, *Corinth*, viii.3: *The Inscriptions, 1926–1950* (Princeton, 1966), 25. For the coin, see K. M. Edwards, *Corinth*, vi: *Coins 1896–1929* (Cambridge, Mass., 1933), 21, no. 47. This coin is recorded in Corinth notebook no. 128, pp. 194–7, as 'found s. end of west line of stones in wall'. In *Corinth*, i.2, the findspot is given as 'on the hardpan near the bottom of the lowest course' of north–south wall associated with Temple E. In this paper, therefore, I do not use the coin as a *terminus ante quem non* for the construction of the first-period temple, but rather as an indication of the date after which the first-phase complex (that is, the south end of the north–south wall, which I identify as the west temenos wall at the back of the early phase of Temple C) was dismantled for a new, second-phase temple. My chronology for the area is as follows: the first Temple E and its temenos wall were constructed before Caligula. The rebuilding with a more generous peristyle was celebrated on the back of the Corinthian duovir's coin, which pictures a hexastyle temple with epistyle inscribed GENT IVLI or AVGVSTVS. The Augustan coin identified as picturing the temple of the Imperial Cult should probably be eliminated from this group; for arguments, see below, note 9. See, also, F. W. Imhoof-Blumer and P. Gardner, *Ancient Coins Illustrating Lost Masterpieces of Greek Art. A Numismatic Commentary on Pausanias* (Chicago, 1964), 22, no. 21, pl. E, xciv. Coin xcv of pl. E should definitely be eliminated from this series, being tetrastyle-prostyle. The Imperial Games are added to the Isthmian calendar under the reign of Tiberius (see Kent, *Corinth*, viii.3, esp. n. 25 on p. 28). The first Temple C and augmented Isthmian games may well be parts of the one overall plan, although there is no archaeological evidence that the first Temple C cannot be earlier.

It should be noted that only two hexastyle temples have yet been excavated near the Roman forum, that of Apollo, cited by Pausanias only as a temple with a statue of Apollo, and Temple E. Temple E in its Flavian state (see below, note 11) carried pedimental sculpture with Imperial iconography, including Apollo and Roma, both statues appropriate for the Imperial Cult. It seems, at the moment, that Temple E is the best candidate yet found in Corinth for the housing of this cult.

I thank M. E. H. Walbank for emphasizing to me the problems that exist concerning Temple E; her conclusions, to appear in dissertation form, and mine, however, have been arrived at independently.

[7] Stillwell *et al.*, *Corinth*, i.2 (see note 6), 166–84. By forcing Pausanias into a rather circuitous exit from the forum, whereby he mounted stairs within the North-west Stoa, Freeman suggests that Temple E might be the Capitolium. Freeman argues that Pausanias would see Temple E only by looking back from East Theatre Street, or from anywhere around Glauke; this cannot stand. The temple was enclosed by a stoa. From the street in front of Glauke, only the roof of Temple E would have been visible over that stoa, and that not necessarily so. Certainly, the roof would have sunk out of sight as one descended the hill along either side of the theatre. Thus, Pausanias would have seen the roof of Temple E, still behind stoas and Glauke, only after he had progressed some distance to the north on the lower plateau of the city and close to the gymnasium, where it would no longer be logical to mention Temple E and a statue of Octavia in any sequential commentary. For what I suggest is the most logical route of Pausanias and disposition of monuments, see C. K. Williams, II, 'Corinth 1974: Forum Southwest', *Hesperia*, xliv (1975), 25–9; C. K. Williams, II, 'Corinth 1983: the route to ikyon', *Hesperia*, liii (1984), 101–4. See G. Roux, *Pausanias en Corinthie*, Annales de l'Université de Lyon, 3rd ser., fasc. xxxi (1958), 112–16 for good analysis of the problem and what I would consider the correct arguments. No longer does archaeological evidence point to a Caligulan date for the construction of the early temple; thus, the initial project may well have been conceived under Tiberius, at which time the 'problem' coin picturing the temple could have been minted. See Prayon below in note 9. See also J. Wiseman, 'Corinth and Rome I: 228 B.C–A.D. 267', *ANRW*, ii.7.2 (1979), 438–548, at 541 (table), for various ideas about the identification of temples around the centre of the Roman city.

[8] The theory here, at least as suggested by the archaeological remains at Corinth, is compatible with the conclusions reached by Price for Asia Minor, because he is speaking of Greek cities, not of Roman colonies. See S. R. F. Price, *Rituals and Power. The Roman Imperial Cult in Asia Minor* (Cambridge, 1984), 165: 'This refutation of the contention that the imperial cult was dominant gives a vivid picture of the continuing vitality of the religious traditions from which the imperial cult derived'.

[9] A series of hexastyle temples with inscribed epistyle appear from Augustus onwards on Corinthian coins. See Imhoof-Blumer and Gardner, *op. cit.* (note 6), para. 21, p. 21. Since this commentary was written Broneer has excavated a peristyle temple to Poseidon with six columns across the front: O. Broneer, *Isthmia*, i: *The Temple of Poseidon* (Princeton, 1971), esp. 101–3. One cannot ignore the possibility that the coin with a hexastyle temple epistyle inscribed CAESAR could have been struck in celebration of the addition of the Caesarea to the Isthmian games. Such an argument may cut into the evidence for the existence of a large peristyle temple in Corinth housing the Imperial Cult almost contemporaneous with the laying out of the city by the Romans. For the theory that a coin may carry an architectural monument even before its dedication, see F. Prayon, 'Projektierte Bauen auf römischen Münzen', *Praestant Interna: Festschrift für Ulrich Hausman*, ed. B. von Freytag Loringhoff *et al.* (Tübingen, 1982), 319–30. Prayon makes a good case for the striking of coins which portray a special building even before its completion. Using this theory one might argue that the earliest Temple E was planned under Augustus, even if not constructed and dedicated until later. No archaeological evidence, however, exists that either of the known hexastyle temples near the forum was in operation under Augustus. See, also, M. J. Price and B. L. Trell, *Coins and their Cities* (London, 1977), 85, for the identification of Temple E on a coin of Caracalla; I do not accept the interpretation of this coin as a depiction of Temple E. The temple is shown as tetrastyle prostyle, not peristyle hexastyle, as the archaeological remains suggest for Temple E. Also, the depiction is that of a symmetrical, colonnaded court, such as the one that enclosed Temple E, not an asymmetrical forum where temples, a fountain and shops with propylon block the direct communication between forum and Temple E. Better is the identification of the temple pictured on the coin of Price and Trell, fig. 143, as Temple E. For the coin evidence affecting the date of Temple E, see above, note 6.

[10] For dating of the first Imperial Games at Isthmia, see Kent, *Corinth*, viii.3 (see note 6), 28, esp. n. 25. See, also, commentary of no. 153, pp. 71–3.

[11] H. S. Robinson, 'A monument of Roma at Corinth', *Hesperia*, xliii (1974), 470–84. Robinson implies

that this monument is late Hadrianic. Kent, *Corinth*, viii.3 (see note 6), 139, no. 352, dates the monument by the epigraphic style of the inscribed names of the hills of Rome 'to the closing years of the first century after Christ'. Indeed, the long-skirted Roma type appears on coins before Hadrian constructs his temple of Venus and Roma with its new cult statue; the evidence provided by the coins might support the Kent date. For a second Roma in Corinth, see F. P. Johnson, *Corinth*, ix: *The Sculpture 1896–1923* (Cambridge, Mass., 1931), 21–2, no. 11, here identified as Enyo or Nike. Concerning the identification, see C. C. Vermeule, *The Goddess Roma in the Art of the Roman Empire* (Cambridge, Mass., 1959; enlarged edn. 1974), 134. Mentioning only that the statue belongs to a group, Vermeule says that its 'presence at Corinth and its Roman imperial (rather than Asia Minor Greek) form stems from the fact the city of Corinth was refounded as a Roman colony'. I associate the Roma statue, S-827, with the pediment group of Temple E in its post-A.D. 79 reconstruction and consider it a necessary part of the functional decoration for a temple of the Imperial Cult. For publication of the pedimental sculpture, see Freeman in *Corinth*, i.2 (see note 6), 210–30. For S-827 see Johnson, *Corinth*, ix (see this note), 21, no. 11.

[12] J. Travlos, *A Pictorial Dictionary of Ancient Athens* (London, 1971), 494, figs. 624–7, with arguments for siting the monument east of the Parthenon. For a variant view, see W. Binder, *Der Roma-Augustus Monopteros auf der Akropolis in Athen und sein topologischer Ort* (Stuttgart, 1969), 45–7, 125.

[13] R. Mellor, *The Worship of the Goddess Roma in the Greek World*, Hypomnemata, xlii (Gottingen, 1975), esp. p. 199.

[14] Pausanias, i.3.7.

[15] H. S. Robinson in *BCH*, ciii (1979), 'Chronique des fouilles et découvertes archéologiques en Grèce en 1978', 550–3 and fig. 65.

[16] C. K. Williams, II, 'Corinth and the Cult of Aphrodite', *Corinthiaca: Studies in Honor of Darrell A. Amyx*, ed. Del Chiaro, University of Missouri Press (in press).

[17] See, especially, the following Corinthian Imperials: Corinth 25.43, bronze of Domitian, A.D. 81–96, Edwards, *Corinth*, vi (see note 6), no. 105, a tetrastyle prostyle temple on a rock. This gives the form of the Aphrodite temple on Akrokorinth. Corinth 13 May 1948, 2, *BMC* 627, bronze of Marcus Aurelius A.D. 161–80. Here the temple in Akrokorinthos is represented as distyle in antis, made so in order to show Aphrodite, standing l., inside. Corinth T26.211a, bronze of Hadrian, A.D. 117–38, see Imhoof-Blumer and Gardner, *op. cit.* (note 6), G cxxi, in which only the statues described by Pausanias are represented. The architectural framework has been eliminated. Examples of and references to this Aphrodite type are collected in *LIMC*, ii.1, 71–3; ii.2, 61–2.

[18] Kent, *Corinth*, viii.3 (see note 6), 123, no. 311.

[19] For Perachora, see R. A. Tomlinson, 'Perachora: the remains outside the two sanctuaries', *BSA*, lxiv (1969), 202–18; for Peirene, see B. H. Hill, *Corinth*, i.6: *The Springs Peirene, Sacred Spring, Glauke* (Princeton, 1964) 15–44.

[20] Kent, *Corinth*, viii.3 (see note 6), 18–19, where Hellenization is clearly visible in the suddenly increasing proportion of Greek to Roman inscriptions in the Hadrianic period. The evidence here is obtained from public inscriptions; but numerous Greek graffiti exist on early Roman pottery from the excavations, signifying a Greek-speaking element within the city. To what extent the language and culture of the indigenous population permeated through the city before encouragement by Nero temporarily, and Hadrian more lastingly, still remains to be determined. For a good thumb-nail commentary on this problem see E. L. Bowie, in his review of Barbara Levick, *Roman Colonies in Southern Asia Minor*, in *JRS*, lx (1970), 206.

[21] Dio Chrysostom, *The Thirty-seventh Discourse: the Corinthian Oration*, trans. H. L. Crosby, Loeb Classical Library (Cambridge, Mass., 1946), 26.

The Design and Planning of Temples and Sanctuaries in Asia Minor in the Roman Imperial Period

Margaret Lyttelton

This paper is intended to be a preliminary discussion of the question to what extent the design and lay-out of certain temples and their sanctuaries in Asia Minor, dating from the Roman Imperial period, were influenced by the architecture and planning of the Imperial Fora in Rome, and by features of the design of Roman temples in general. In this necessarily brief survey only a selection of the most important temples of the Roman Imperial period in Asia Minor can be considered, so that this inquiry cannot be regarded as exhaustive, and the conclusions reached must be seen as somewhat speculative. Indeed, it would be rash to offer more than a tentative view of this whole question of the influence of Rome on the sanctuaries of Asia Minor while so much relevant archaeological work is still in progress on the sites, or remains to be undertaken.[1] There is the obvious danger in making generalizations about the architectural style of fashions in planning evident in the sanctuaries of Asia Minor that they may at any time be modified, or even overturned, by the discovery of fresh and unsuspected evidence. Nevertheless, it seems worthwhile to make the attempt, however hazardous, to trace the extent of the influence of the architectural style of Rome on the design and layout of sanctuaries in Asia Minor, which, being one of the eastern provinces, was a previously Hellenized area, in which Hellenistic traditions and conventions were deeply rooted. 'For there should be more to architectural history than the counting of columns and measuring of stylobates', as Simon Price has aptly remarked.[2]

Before considering the specific question of Roman architectural influence in the province of Asia Minor, it seems appropriate to look at the general impact of Roman intervention in this area under the empire. As is well known, the most far-reaching effect of Roman imperial rule on the provincial towns of the east of the empire, particularly in Asia Minor, was to restore peace, and with it prosperity. Numerous inscriptions testify to these eastern cities' gratitude for the restoration of peace to the Roman world by Augustus, for a favourable economic climate is an essential pre-requisite for any substantial building programme, such as the construction of many of the large-scale temples and sanctuaries built in Asia Minor in the first two centuries of the Imperial period.[3]

Roman patronage also, both imperial and private, was an important element in the architectural scene in Asia Minor in the first two centuries A.D. The courting of public renown by private individuals as well as by emperors, and the characteristics of self-confidence and even self-advertisement of these Roman patrons seem to find reflec-tion in the grandiose architectural style, and the exuberantly carved architectural decoration of many buildings of Asia Minor in the Imperial period. The magnificent Temple of 'Hadrian' at Cyzicus, which was in fact probably dedicated to Zeus, was erected in part at the expense of the emperor Hadrian, while the ornate little Temple of Hadrian at Ephesus was dedicated by a private citizen. It is now argued that this temple was dedicated to Artemis as well as Hadrian.[4]

A number of the temples to be considered in this brief survey of the sanctuaries of Asia Minor in the Roman period were built for the Imperial Cult; new cults like that of the emperor, or those of the 'Oriental' deities—the so-called Mystery religions—required the provision of new buildings. So, for example, we find a Temple of Roma and Augustus at Ankara, and the Temple of Domitian and the Temple of Serapis at Ephesus. Surprisingly, these new cults did not apparently show any consistency in the type of sanctuaries which their devotees erected in the various cities of Asia Minor. The choice of the type of temple, or sanctuary building and its setting, seems to have been eclectic and arbitrary, taken now from Roman, and now from Hellenistic, models. So, for example, the Temple of Trajan on the Acropolis at Pergamum (fig. 6, 3), although it is a peripteral temple of Hellenistic type, shows clear signs of influences from Rome. For it is built in the Corinthian order, and stands on a podium of Roman type approached up a staircase at the front only. The temple is set in a temenos, or court, exactly on its axis, and is flanked on three sides by colonnades. This temple, constructed on an imposing scale, set on a podium, and framed by a colonnaded court, owes something to Roman architectural concepts and planning; to a considerable extent it appears to be modelled on the Temple of Mars Ultor in the Forum of Augustus in Rome (fig. 2, p. 8).[5]

However, the design of the Temple of Hadrian at Ephesus is derived from eastern, rather than western, architectural traditions, for it has an arched entablature framed by a triangular pediment as the central feature of its façade. This decorative design derives not from the architecture of Rome, but from that of Syria of the late Hellenistic period. For the Temple of Dushara at the Nabataean sanctuary of Si' in the Hauran, dating from the later first century B.C., apparently had an arched entablature spanning the central intercolumniation of the façade, which was set beneath a raking cornice giving the effect of a pediment.[6] Similarly, with temples dedicated to the relatively new Oriental cults, models for the design followed appear to have been indiscriminately taken from the traditions of the eastern Hellenistic world, or from that of Imperial Rome. The Temple of Serapis at Ephesus is a building in traditional Roman style, being a prostyle temple set on a podium, and axially

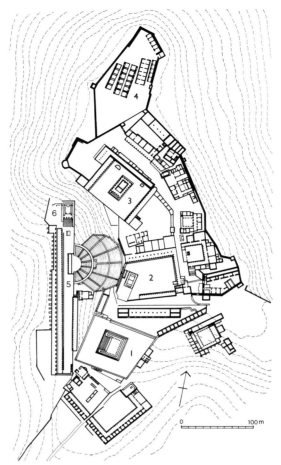

FIG. 6. Plan of the Acropolis at Pergamum (from Lyttelton, *op. cit.* (note 6), fig. 31; figs. 6–8 here reproduced by courtesy of Thames and Hudson)

approached through a propylon and colonnaded court.[7] In contrast, the much larger sanctuary of Serapis at Pergamum is of a highly unconventional, un-Roman design. Constructed in the third century A.D. of red brick faced with marble, this was the largest building in ancient Pergamum. It consisted of a central hall in the form of a basilica with a nave and two aisles, which was flanked on the two long sides by a pair of square colonnaded courts, each of which opened into a domed rotunda on its east side. West of these three buildings lay a vast rectangular court, under which the river Selinus flowed in two vaulted tunnels. Here, perhaps, Egyptian influences can be detected.[8]

Predictably, new or rebuilt temples dedicated to age-old deities like Zeus were usually of conventional form. Thus, the Temple of Zeus at Aezani is a pseudo-dipteral Ionic building, although it has some anomalous features, and the Temple of Zeus at Euromus is a peripteral building of the Corinthian order, set on a stylobate.[9] As these examples make clear, Roman architectural influence was not strongly felt everywhere in Asia Minor, even by the end of the first century A.D.

We may now consider in detail a number of other temples erected in Asia Minor in the first and second centuries A.D., in order to see to what extent Roman influence can be traced in their architectural style, and in the design of sanctuaries in general. Two of the earliest temples in the area dating from the Imperial period are the Temple of Augustus and Roma at Ankara, and that of Augustus and (?)Men at Pisidian Antioch. These two temples in fact form an interesting contrast in respect of Roman influence, for the temple erected at Pisidian Antioch, where a Roman colony was founded around 25 B.C., overlying a Hellenistic settlement, displays strong signs of influence from Rome. This temple (fig. 7, 1) is a prostyle-tetrastyle building of the Corinthian order; it stands on a high podium and is approached, at the front only, by an impressive flight of steps.[10] Moreover, this temple does not stand in isolation like the traditional Hellenistic or Greek peripteral temples of Asia Minor, such as the Temple of Athena Polias at Priene.[11] The temple at Pisidian Antioch was set on a commanding hillside site, and framed by a two-storey portico, which ran round in a semicircle behind the temple, close to its rear wall, cutting back into the hillside as it did so. The lower order of this colonnade was apparently Doric, while the upper order was Ionic. A rather similar curved colonnade frames the Temple of Juno Caelestis at Dougga in Tunisia. Here, it has been suggested that the semicircular form of the colonnade was dictated by the lunar aspect of Tanit, the local goddess with whom Juno was associated. So at Pisidian Antioch the curved colonnade might be taken as

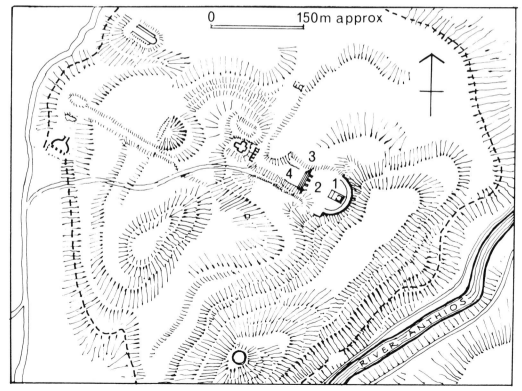

Fig. 7. Sketch plan of Pisidian Antioch (from Lyttelton, *op. cit.* (note 6), fig. 34)

support for the suggestion, recently contested, that the temple was dedicated to Men, an Anatolian moon god.[12]

In front of the Temple of Augustus at Pisidian Antioch there was a large paved terrace named as the Augusta Platea in an inscription. At the edge of this terrace, on the axis of the temple, an arched gateway was later added to this architectural ensemble. Immediately below the site of this later gateway, still on the axis of the temple, a large flight of steps led down to another paved terrace. This was known as the Platea Tiberia, and was presumably added to the temple complex in Tiberius' reign. So here the same axis was preserved through an impressive sequence of terraces, steps and temple, framed by a semicircular colonnade.[13] This complex, or others like it now unknown, may have had some influence on the planning of the great sanctuaries of Artemis at Jerash (fig. 8) and the Temple of Jupiter Heliopolitanus at Baalbek,[14] both largely of the second century A.D., anticipating, as it does, their use of axial planning and a framework of colonnades to create a unified architectural ensemble centring on the temple. The axial plan of the Temple of Augustus was most

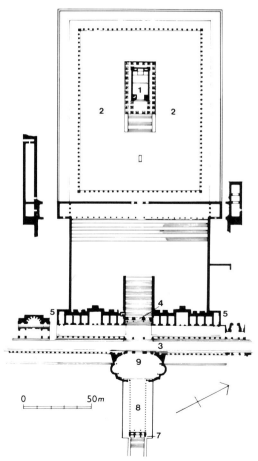

FIG. 8. Plan of the Sanctuary of Artemis at Jerash (from Lyttelton, *op. cit.* (note 6), fig. 37)

probably derived from the axial plan of the Temple of Mars Ultor (fig. 2, p. 8), which was dedicated in 2 B.C., but was begun rather earlier, having been vowed in 42 B.C.[15]

We may note, however, that there are still some features in the temple at Pisidian Antioch which are a Hellenistic legacy, rather than a contemporary influence from Rome. The temple is only framed, not completely enclosed, by the curved colonnade. This scheme echoes the Hellenistic tradition of framing buildings with stoas, rather than completely encircling them with a peristyle court, as became the fashion in Roman architecture.[16] Indicative, too, of the Hellenistic background is the mixture of the orders: Corinthian for the temple, and Doric and Ionic for the semicircular colonnade. Roman architectural taste demanded uniformity in the choice of the architectural order. Hence, in the Imperial Fora in Rome the temples and their surrounding colonnades are all of the Corinthian order.

By contrast, the Temple of Augustus and Roma at Ankara, which was probably built *c.* 25 B.C. after the annexation of Galatia by Augustus, is a building much more fully in the Hellenistic tradition—so much so that the temple was once thought to have

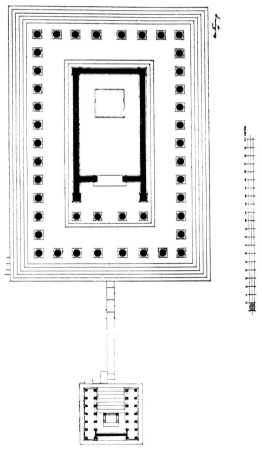

FIG. 9. Reconstructed ground plan of the Temple of Domitian at Ephesus (from *JÖAI*, xxvii (1932), fig. 37)

been constructed in the second century B.C.[17] The temple stands on a stylobate, rather than a podium, which is of considerable size, measuring 36 by 55 m. The temple had a pseudo-dipteral plan, with eight columns across the front and rear, and fifteen down the sides. This type of plan was popularized by the architect Hermogenes in the second century B.C. in the Temple of Artemis at Magnesia on the Maeander.[18] Within the peristyle colonnade, the temple has a prostyle porch of four Corinthian columns, while the opisthodomos at the rear has two columns in antis, which were also probably of the Corinthian order. Use of the Corinthian order was probably a concession to Roman taste.

The Temple of Domitian at Ephesus (fig. 9) has a very similar plan, although it is built on a much smaller scale, and is without an opisthodomos. This temple was built in the emperor's lifetime by the citizens of Ephesus, but was rededicated to Vespasian and the Flavian Gens after Domitian's murder in A.D. 96.[19] This temple, although relatively small, occupies a dominating position in the town plan of Ephesus, for it is built on a high artifical platform to face east across the State Agora, although the temple was not set on the axis of the agora. However, the altar in front of the temple was set on the long axis of the temple. The terrace on which the temple stood was artificially raised well above the level of the agora. The raised terrace measured 50 by 100 m. and was approached up steps, and encircled by colonnades which formed a frame for the temple. In contrast with the imposing size of the supporting terrace, the temple itself was quite small, measuring 24 by 34 m. on the stylobate. In plan the temple was pseudo-dipteral, and had a prostyle porch of four columns. In Byzantine times the temple was converted into a cistern, no doubt making use of its commanding height; most of the architectural features of the temple seem to have been destroyed in the course of this transformation.[20]

Another important and significant temple built in Asia Minor in the Imperial period is the Temple of Zeus at Aezani (fig. 10) in Phrygia, on the Anatolian plateau. The exact date of this temple is uncertain: the evidence of coins and inscriptions can be adduced to support either a Flavian or a Hadrianic date.[2] This imposing marble temple stands on a many-stepped stylobate, which is of an impressive size, measuring 33 by 37 m. The temple is pseudo-dipteral in plan, and has a prostyle porch of four columns; the plan is therefore similar to that of the temple at Ankara discussed above. The columns of the peristyle are Ionic, while those of the porch are of the Composite order. At the rear of the cella there is an opisthodomos with two columns in antis preceding it. From the opisthodomos flights of steps lead down to a vaulted chamber.[22] This has been taken to be a sign of Roman architectural influence, but the chamber appears rather to have been built to house the local cult of Mater Steunene, which down to the second century A.D. was practised in a cave just outside Aezani.[23] Thus, this temple, with its pseudo-dipteral plan and Ionic order, can be seen to have been influenced by the style of Asia Minor in the Hellenistic period, rather than by the architectural conventions of Rome. However, in its setting the Temple of Zeus at Aezani can be seen to have owed something to Roman concepts of planning as exemplified in the Imperial Fora (fig. 2, p. 8). For the temple at Aezani was set in a colonnaded court, on its long axis, while the approach from the agora to the court was through a gateway on the same axis.[24]

It is particularly difficult to disentangle the architectural influences at work on the grandiose 'Temple of Hadrian' at Cyzicus, as it is now known only from the remains of its substructures, and copies of drawings by Cyriaco da Ancona. Cyriaco visited the

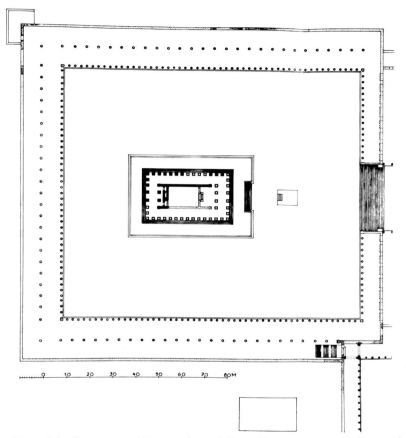

FIG. 10. Plan of the Sanctuary of Zeus at Aezani (from Neumann, *op. cit.* (note 21), pl. 4)

temple in 1431 and 1444, when thirty-one columns of this vast temple, known in antiquity as one of the Wonders of the World, were still standing.[25] The temple apparently had a peristyle of eight by fifteen columns, as did the temples at Aezani and Ankara, but it was probably peripteral, rather than pseudo-dipteral in plan like them, although this is not recorded by Cyriaco.[26] The order of the temple was Corinthian, or at least a variant Corinthian form. Cyriaco shows a number of Corinthianizing columns with shafts decorated with a criss-cross pattern of vine leaves and grapes. These columns may represent the interior order of the temple. Further drawings show similar columns supporting arched architraves; these may represent part of a forecourt as the larger columns of the temple appear to rise up behind the arcade. This appears to be the earliest recorded use of an arcade on columns in monumental architecture. On a domestic scale arcades are depicted in Pompeian frescoes, and survive in the peristyle of the Casa della Fortuna at Pompeii.[27]

Although the plan of this temple may have been derived from the Hellenistic architecture of Asia Minor, yet its exuberant decoration seems to reflect specifically Roman tastes. The elaborate carving is reminiscent of the florid decoration of many of the buildings of the Flavian period in Rome, while the use of Corinthian, or Corinthianizing, columns apparently throughout the building complex is, as we shall see, a characteristic feature of the large-scale building complexes comprising the Imperial Fora in Rome.[28]

The temple at Ephesus now generally agreed to have been dedicated to Serapis (fig. 11), perhaps rather surprisingly shows both in its design and in the general lay-out of the temenos, or sanctuary, more of the architectural influence of Rome than any of the other temples considered in this survey. For in this sanctuary of an Oriental deity eastern, rather than western, architectural traditions might have been expected to be evident. The Temple of Serapis was built on the west side of the commercial agora at Ephesus during the second century A.D. It is a prostyle temple, set on a high podium, with eight monolithic columns, 15 m. high, running across the façade to form a porch, which was approached up a flight of steps.[29] The order of the columns was Corinthian. A door 5 m. wide led into the cella, which was 29 m. deep, and roofed by a vault. The temple stood against the centre of the rear wall of a rectangular precinct, which was bordered by colonnades. The court was entered from the street up a flight of steps leading through a gateway set on the axis of the temple. This prostyle, Corinthian temple, standing on a podium, and axially approached through a gateway

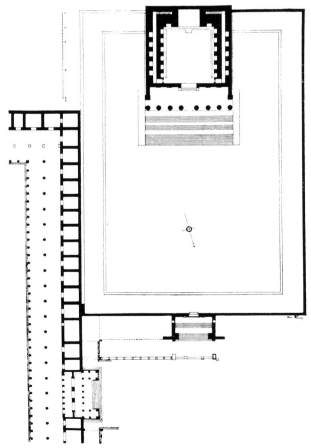

FIG. 11. Plan of the Sanctuary of Serapis at Ephesus (from *JÖAI*, xxiii (1928), fig. 53)

and colonnaded court, appears to be modelled on the plan of the Imperial Fora in Rome (fig. 2, p. 8), where temples are axially set in colonnaded courts, and in some instances are axially approached.

Axial planning increasingly becomes a feature of the sanctuaries of Asia Minor in the Imperial period. In the Temple of Serapis at Ephesus the axial plan is carried right through the approach to the temple and the temple in its court, as was also the case with the Temple of Zeus at Aezani, while the Temple of Trajan at Pergamum (fig. 6) was axially set in a colonnaded court, although not axially approached. Furthermore, the Temple of Augustus at Pisidian Antioch was axially approached up flights of steps (fig. 7), although it was not entirely surrounded by a colonnaded court, as was the case with the temples in the Imperial Fora in Rome. The Romans did not invent the concept of axial planning, which can be traced back to Hellenistic building complexes, like the Temple of Asclepius at Cos, and perhaps further back to Egyptian models.[30] In fact, there evolved and came to fruition in Roman Imperial times a radically different conception of planning from that followed by the Greeks.[31] For in a Roman town the important buildings were not seen in isolation, and as separate independent masses, but rather as parts of a greater whole. Hence the tendency of Roman town planning was to establish links between buildings by means of colonnades, flights of steps, and an axially organized approach (fig. 2, p. 8). This type of planning can be seen in the Imperial Fora in Rome, and in the eastern provinces in the Temple of Jupiter Heliopolitanus at Baalbek, and the Temple of Artemis at Jerash (fig. 8).[32] Thus, eventually, in a Roman town almost all the buildings became enclosed and inward-looking. Markets became vast enclosed courts, while temples were also enclosed by colonnaded courts on all sides, as in the Imperial Fora, and the Temple of Serapis and that of Domitian at Ephesus. And so we find, appropriately, the growth of the Roman taste for the Corinthian order, to the virtual exclusion of the other orders, for the decorative and versatile Corinthian order seems to have been developed in Greece in the course of the fourth century B.C. in response to the difficulties found in articulating building interiors with columns.[33] When major sanctuaries became, in the Roman Imperial period, virtually enclosed spaces, with much of the architectural character of an interior, it was appropriate that they should make use of the Corinthian order, which was so well suited to use in interiors, being of more slender proportions and more easily sliced into half columns and pilasters than the Doric or Ionic.[34] The Corinthian order also obviously responded to the Roman taste for the ornate and grandiose, so its widespread use in the temples of Asia Minor of Roman Imperial date considered in this survey is one element of their architectural design which can almost certainly be derived from Roman models.

For the most part, however, there was, as far as this survey indicates, no wholesale adoption of Roman architectural precedents or following of Roman models in the design and layout of sanctuaries in Asia Minor in the first and second centuries A.D. It is particularly interesting, therefore, to note that Asia Minor, with her long history of Hellenization and rich resources of available marble, developed an independent school of marble carving for the decoration of building façades. This is evident in such details as the precise sequence of mouldings almost invariably used on entablatures, such as the architrave crown of an astragal, ovolo and cavetto, or the ovolo carved on the cornice around the edge of the modillions, and in the particular forms of the decorated mouldings used, such as variants of the usual leaf ornament of the cyma reversa moulding.[35] Thus, in Asia Minor a style of architectural carving was developed which was rather different from that practised in Rome. Indeed, on some Hadrianic buildings in Rome, such as the Temple of Venus and Rome, which were constructed of Proconnesian marble, the fact that marble-cutters were imported from Asia Minor to carve this marble can be detected from the sequences of mouldings used on the entablatures, and from the style of the mouldings themselves, which all reflect the usages of the craftsmen of Asia Minor. Evolving from the traditions of the Hellenistic period, Asia Minor to a large extent developed an independent architectural style. In certain ways, however, particularly in the imposition of axial planning, and in the increasingly exclusive use of the Corinthian order, the influence of the architectural style of Rome on that of Asia Minor can be clearly seen. Yet in other respects, such as the continuing preference for free-standing peripteral temples, the traditional architectural conventions of the Hellenistic period continued to hold sway in Asia Minor in the Imperial period.

NOTES

[1] For example, S. Mitchell's new survey of Pisidian Antioch is not yet fully published (see below, note 10), and K. Erim's excavations are still in progress at Aphrodisias. Remote sites like Adada and Kanytelis have extensive, but little studied, remains, which may include significant buildings (information from H. Brewster).

[2] In *JRS*, lxxii (1982), 197.

[3] For example, inscription from Halicarnassus (British Museum Greek Insc. no. 854) cited in K. Hopkins, *Conquerors and Slaves* (Cambridge, 1978), 217. R. Martin, *L'Urbanisme dans la Grèce antique* (Paris, 1974), 183.

[4] For the probable dedication of the Temple of Hadrian at Cyzicus to Zeus, see S. Price, *Rituals and Power* (Cambridge, 1984), 153–6, 251–2. See also D. Magie, *Roman Rule in Asia Minor* (Princeton, 1950), ii, 1472–3. For the Temple of Hadrian at Ephesus see F. Miltner in *JÖAI*, xliv (1959), Beibl. 264–6; Price, *op. cit.*, 149–50, 255–6.

[5] For the Trajaneum see *AvPerg* (1895), v.2, and for the Imperial Fora, A. Boëthius and J. Ward-Perkins, *Etruscan and Roman Architecture* (Harmondsworth, 1970), 190–1. Ward-Perkins (*op. cit.*, 266) draws attention to the fact that workmen from Asia Minor, perhaps from the Trajaneum, were employed on Hadrian's Temple of Venus and Rome, in Rome, which was constructed of Proconnesian marble. See further D. Strong in *PBSR*, xxi (1953), 133. See also Price, *op. cit.* (note 4), 156, 252.

[6] See H. C. Butler, *Princeton Archaeological Expeditions to Syria* (Leiden, 1906–19), ii.A, 385 and fig. 329. See also M. Lyttelton, *Baroque Architecture in Classical Antiquity* (London, 1974), 260–1.

[7] See further, pp. 46–7.

[8] E. Boehringer in *Neue deutsche Ausgrabungen im Mittelmeergebiet und im vorderen Orient* (Berlin, 1959), 136–8.

[9] E. Akurgal, *Ancient Civilizations and Ruins of Turkey* (Istanbul, 1978), 246, fig. 93. The temple has six columns on the façades, and eleven down the sides. The stylobate measures 14·4 by 26·8 m.

[10] D. Robinson in *Art Bulletin*, ix (1926), 11–19, and *AJA*, xxviii (1924), 437–42. For preliminary accounts of the new survey see S. Mitchell in *AS*, xxxiii (1983), 9–11, and xxxiv (1984), 8–10. Price, *op. cit.* (note 4), 269–70. Mitchell rejects the recent suggestion that this temple was dedicated to Cybele and Men, and considers that the most plausible dedication is to Augustus.

[11] T. Wiegand and H. Schrader, *Priene* (Berlin, 1904), 128–9.

[12] A. Golfetto, *Dougga* (Basle, 1962), 41–3, fig. 8. For a sanctuary to the moon god, Men, near Pisidian Antioch, see M. Hardie in *JHS*, xxxii (1912), 111–50.

[13] See note 10, and Lyttelton, *op. cit.* (note 6), 213. Magie, *op. cit.* (note 4), 1319–20.

[14] For Jerash, see Martin, *op. cit.* (note 3), 179–80, and for Baalbek, T. Wiegand, *Baalbek* (Berlin, 1921), i, plates, and i, text, for Jupiter temple. See also Lyttelton, *op. cit.* (note 6), 216–22.

[15] Boëthius and Ward-Perkins, *op. cit.* (note 5), 190.

[16] See further, p. 47, and J. Coulton, *The Architectural Development of the Greek Stoa* (Oxford, 1976), 168–9.

[17] D. Krencker and M. Schede, *Der Tempel in Ankara* (Berlin and Leipzig, 1936). For the date see E. Wiegand in *Gnomon*, xiii (1937), 414–22. Price, *op. cit.* (note 4), 267–8.

[18] A. W. Lawrence, *Greek Architecture* (Harmondsworth, 1957), 216–17, with refs., fig. 120.

[19] For the dedication see Price, *op. cit.* (note 4), 255, with refs. For a description J. Keil in *JÖAI*, xxvii (1932), Beibl. 52–60.

[20] C. Foss, *Ephesus after Antiquity* (Cambridge, 1979), 134.

[21] R. Naumann, *Der Zeustempel zu Aizanoi* (Berlin, 1979). Reviewed by Price, *loc. cit.* (note 2), 196–7.

[22] Naumann, *op. cit.* (note 21), pls. 10, 11.

[23] Price, *loc. cit.* (note 2), 196–7. L. Robert in *BCH*, cv (1981), 331–60.

[24] Naumann, *op. cit.* (note 21), 45 ff., pls. 3, 4.

[25] B. Ashmole, *Journal of the Warburg and Courtauld Institutes*, xix (1956), 179–90, pls. 34–39. Price, *op. cit.* (note 4), 153–6 and 251–2, argues that this temple was dedicated not to Hadrian, but to Zeus.

[26] Ashmole, *loc. cit.* (note 25), 182–3.

[27] A. Boëthius, *The Golden House of Nero* (Ann Arbor, 1960), 74; Lyttelton, *op. cit.* (note 6), 261–2.

[28] See p. 47.

[29] J. Keil in *JÖAI*, xxiii (1926), Beibl. 266–70, fig. 53. It was not at first recognized as a Serapaeum. See now W. Alzinger in *RE*, Suppl. xii (1970), 1653, and G. Hölbl, *Zeugnisse ägyptischer Religionsvorstellungen für Ephesus* (Leiden, 1978), 33–7, fig. 2.

[30] Coulton, *op. cit.* (note 16), 170–2.

[31] Martin, *op. cit.* (note 3), 79, and Coulton, *op. cit.* (note 16), 168.

[32] See note 14.

[33] G. Roux, *L'Architecture de l'Argolide* (Paris, 1961), 373, 383–8.

[34] Roux, *op. cit.* (note 33), 387.

[35] Strong, *loc. cit.* (note 5), 131 ff, and Lyttelton, *op. cit.* (note 6), 271–2.

Imperial Bath Buildings in South-West Asia Minor

Andrew Farrington

The bath buildings of south-west Asia Minor display a great variety of forms which is part of the wider architectural diversity to be seen in this province.[1] From this variety emerge four more or less clearly defined types of building, although a significant number of baths in south-west Asia Minor lie outside these typological groupings: (1) the bath–gymnasium complex and related buildings; (2) bath buildings based essentially on a row arrangement; (3) bath buildings based essentially on a block arrangement; (4) bath buildings with a central rectangular covered gallery.

1. The bath-complex and related buildings[2]

At a number of sites is to be seen a thermal establishment, highly complex in plan, but consisting of two main architectural elements, the bath block and the palaestra, to which equal attention is devoted. Of this group of buildings, the Gymnasium at Sardis (early third century A.D.), the Gymnasium at Alexandria Troas (early second century A.D.), and the Ephesian East Gymnasium (early second century A.D.), Theatre Gymnasium (second century A.D.), and Gymnasium of Vedius (mid-second century A.D.), form a smaller group which displays a large number of common features.[3]

The bath block consists of a sequence of the usual rooms to be found in a bath building, namely apodyterium, caldarium, tepidarium and frigidarium, and occasionally natationes (plunge or swimming pools). These elements are disposed symmetrically about a central axis. Intercommunicating with the bath block by means of a number of rooms along the edge of the bath block is a palaestra which is often surrounded by rooms facing into and accessible from the palaestra. The palaestra is entered by a monumental propylon. The Ephesian Gymnasium of Vedius displays this plan in its clearest form (fig. 12). At the eastern end of the complex stands the palaestra, which is entered by an impressive propylon. Within, rooms stand on at least three sides of the palaestra. A common feature of this group of buildings, but one for which the ancient name and precise role has yet to be discovered, the so-called

'Kaisersaal',[4] is flanked by two rooms which communicate with the first room of the bath block proper. Beyond this lies a piered gallery which communicates with a long narrow frigidarium and pair of apodyteria set on either side of the frigidarium. Beyond this the whole of the west end of the bath block is occupied by the caldarium range.

The bath–gymnasium complexes of Ephesus, Sardis, and Alexandria Troas form a group whose plans show little variation. Outside this small subgroup, our otherwise varied bath buildings display the distinguishing feature of a rectangular plan set symmetrically about the short axis of the rectangle. This type of symmetrical plan, in varying degrees of simplicity and sophistication, is to be seen in the sprawling Harbour Baths at Ephesus (orignally Domitianic), the so-called 'Terme Extra Muros' at Hierapolis in Phrygia (third centry A.D.), in the as yet unpublished 'Gymnasium of Hadrian' at Laodicea ad Lycum, also in Phrygia (*c.* A.D. 129), and in the 'Baths of Hadrian' at Aphrodisias in Caria (*c.* A.D. 129). Restricted generally to south-west Asia Minor, this symmetry of plan is also to be seen in the Gymnasium at distant Aezani (second century A.D.), and in the 'Baths of Caracalla' at Ankara (A.D. 211–17).[5]

2. *Bath buildings based essentially on a row arrangement*

A bath of the 'row-type', to borrow the old, but still useful, terminology of a pioneering study of Roman baths, consists of a series of rectangular rooms, usually three, on parallel axes, occasionally with an apse set in the short wall of one of the outer rooms and containing a basin. This is a standard pattern for smaller baths throughout the empire, and is subject to a large number of variations. In south-west Asia Minor, the plan is to be found mainly in Lycia, where it occurs with almost

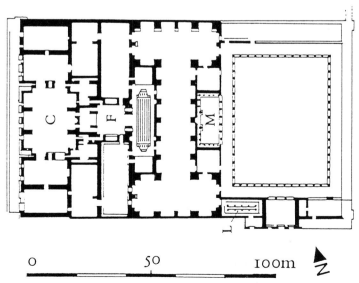

FIG. 12. Plan of the Gymnasium of Vedius at Ephesus (after Ward-Perkins, *op. cit.* (note 1), 293, by courtesy of B. R. Ward-Perkins)

monotonous uniformity in all the major cities and there are at least twenty-four examples still surviving (figs. 13 and 14). Most are dated to between about A.D. 70 and 150. Occasionally another room is set at right-angles to the row of three rooms. An apse sometimes projects from one of the short walls of a room, and a palaestra sometimes adjoins the bath block.

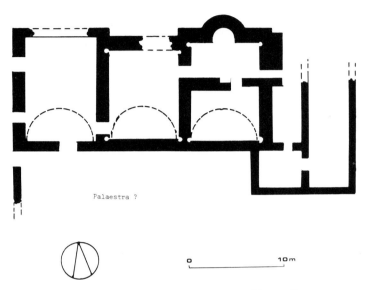

FIG. 13. Plan of the Baths of Antoninus Pius at Cyaneae

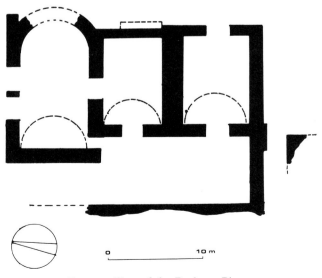

FIG. 14. Plan of the Baths at Pinara

The plan is found again in a clear local variant in Cilicia, at Anemourium, Antiochia and Cragum, Iotape, and Syedra (all first to second century A.D.), and in a monumentalized and less rigid form in the unpublished 'North Baths' at Laodicea ad Lycum (second century A.D.) and Great Baths at Tripolis, both in Phrygia, and in the South Gymnasium at Perge and the baths at Sillyum, both in Pamphylia.[6]

3. *Baths based essentially on a block arrangement*

It was pointed out at the end of the last century that smaller Roman baths are occasionally organized on a square or rectangular grid plan.[7] This rectangular arrangement informs one or two baths in south-west Asia Minor, and is to be seen in the possibly Severan North Baths at Perge, in the 'Stadionthermen' at Selge in Pisidia (second century A.D.), and in the Milesian Baths of Capito (A.D. 43) (fig. 15). The block arrangement is even clearer in the tiny Baths of Titus at Simena in Lycia (A.D. 80), and in the unpublished Late Baths at Corasium in Rough Cilicia (third to fourth century A.D.). The number of baths on a block arrangement so far discovered does not form a significant proportion of the total number of known bath buildings in south-west Asia Minor, and it is only their underlying regularity of plan which makes them a small, if noticeable, group.[8]

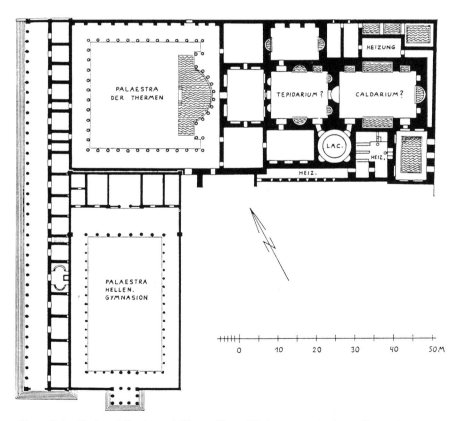

FIG. 15. Plan of the Baths of Capito at Miletus (from Kleiner, *op. cit.* (note 8), 99, here reproduced by courtesy of De Gruyter)

4. Bath buildings with a central rectangular gallery

The plan of this type of bath building consists of a series of rooms organized round a central rectangular gallery. This central chamber gives access on to all the surrounding chambers. At the far end of the gallery of the Baths II.7.a at Anemourium, and of the baths at Syedra, a square pool has been found (fig. 16). The plan of this group of baths is clear and distinct, and is restricted to eastern Pamphylia and Rough Cilicia.[9]

In south-west Asia Minor, then, the Imperial bath building displays several notably different types of plan, which are, furthermore, quite strictly limited to certain areas. The bath-gymnasium complex is scarcely to be found outside the western coastlands of Asia Minor, the highly standardized three-chamber 'row-type' plan is not to be found with such uniformity outside Lycia and Cilicia, and the bath organized round a central gallery is not, as far as I know, to be found outside eastern Pamphylia and Rough Cilicia.

Are any of these baths the product of the continuity of Hellenistic bathing traditions into Imperial times? Are they the product of Rome and Italy merely transported into the East? Or are any of them the local Imperial answer to the spread of highly sophisticated Roman bathing habits?

Few enough Hellenistic baths have so far been excavated anywhere, and only one has come to light in south-west Asia Minor, at Colophon. There is, as far as I know, so far only one epigraphical reference to a Hellenistic bath in Lycia, where bathing was

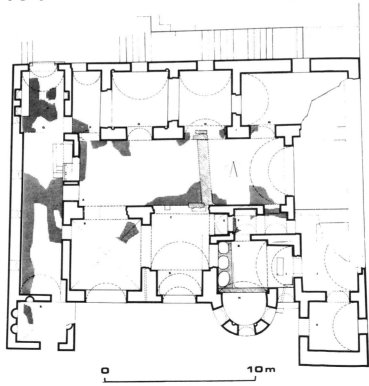

0   10m

FIG. 16. Plan of Baths II.7.a at Anemourium (after Rosenbaum *et al.*, *op. cit.* (note 6), 5, by courtesy of Türk Tarih Kurumu)

apparently so popular in later, Imperial, times.[10] Hellenistic baths would have appeared to consist of circular rooms lined with basins in which all or most of the washing was performed. Archaeological remains suggest that the complicated bathing sequences beloved of the Romans, and requiring different heating temperatures, were perhaps invented in southern Italy, in the second century B.C. Certainly there are, in the writings of those from whom we would most expect them, no Greek equivalents or originals for the Latin terms for the different rooms of a Roman bath.[11]

Nothing in or around Asia Minor offers us buildings similar to and earlier than those we have already considered. We therefore turn to Rome and Italy in the hope of finding prototypes of any of these buildings of Imperial Asia Minor.

At Pompeii, in Campania, three sets of baths, the Stabian Baths (second century B.C. and after) (fig. 17), the Forum Baths (80 B.C.), and the Central Baths (A.D. 63–79), strongly resemble the three-chambered baths of Lycia. This type of layout is not restricted to Campania, although these baths at Pompeii appear to be the earliest examples of their type. Baths with similar plans are to be seen in Rome and Italy up to the beginning of the third century A.D. Similar plans are to be seen, too, throughout the northern part of the Empire, in Britain, France and Germany.[12]

Similar as these Italian plans are to the plans of some baths in Lycia and Rough Cilicia, the plans of Lycian and Cilician baths have been somewhat simplified. The circular rooms of the Pompeian baths, which may have held the hot dry laconicum, are generally absent from baths in south-west Asia Minor, suggesting that this part of the bathing routine was not favoured. One or two Lycian baths, moreover, seem originally to have consisted of only two rooms, only one of which was heated. The bathing pattern employed in these small baths may have been nearer to that of a

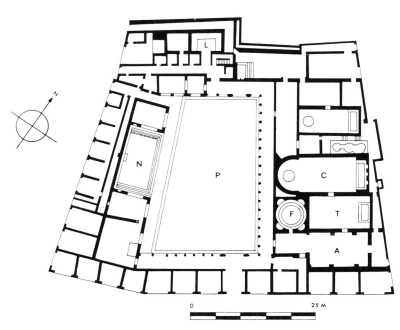

FIG. 17. Plan of the Stabian Baths at Pompeii (from F. Sear, *Roman Architecture* (1982), 40, here reproduced by courtesy of Batsford)

Hellenistic bath than to the sequential patterns of three-chambered Roman baths of Italy.

Italy provides us with prototypes of two regional groups of baths of south-west Asia Minor. It also provides the model for the bath–gymnasium complex and related buildings. The inspiration for these buildings lies in the Imperial thermae of Rome, the sequence of great bathing establishments built by various emperors. We can trace the line of development from the Baths of Agrippa (25 B.C.), through the Baths of Nero, Trajan and Caracalla (fig. 18), to the Baths of Diocletian and, ultimately, of Constantine. These plans are characterized by a double and symmetrical circulatory pattern. The axiality of the plan is firmly emphasized, with a clear single passage from the caldarium range, through a small tepidarium, into the area of the frigidarium and natatio.[13]

The plan of the Gymnasium of Vedius at Ephesus (fig. 12) is informed by a rather differently distributed symmetry, and by a different emphasis accorded to component rooms of the bath block. In particular, there is no longer the strong axial emphasis through the centre of the bath block. The caldarium no longer projects, and there is no longer an emphatic distinction between the rooms in the caldarium range. The frigidarium has shrunk in size, but the colonnaded courtyard of the thermae is accorded greater importance in the overall design.

These changes, presumably caused by different bathing tastes, mean that the relationship between these bath–gymnasium complexes and the thermae of Rome is considerably less close than that between the smaller baths of Italy and the baths of Lycia. The other more loosely related members of this group display their only similarity to the Imperial thermae in their symmetrical plan, and occasionally projecting caldarium. There is only one bath known in south-west Asia Minor, in which the

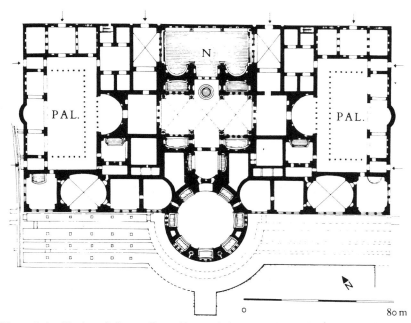

FIG. 18. Plan of the Baths of Caracalla at Rome (after Ward-Perkins, *op. cit.* (note 1), 131, by courtesy of B. R. Ward-Perkins)

influence of the Imperial thermae is markedly more strong than anywhere else: the baths at Caunus. Unique, so far as I know, is the emphasis on the clear passage along the short axis of the building. A glance outside Asia Minor, at North African or German baths, show how much more closely these baths are related to Imperial thermae. The North Baths at Timgad (third century A.D.), the Antonine Baths at Carthage (A.D. 143–62), the baths at Cuicul in North Africa, and the 'Kaiserthermen' at Trier (fourth century A.D.) all display an emphasis upon the central axis which brings them closer to the Imperial thermae than anything in south-west Asia Minor. Yeğül has shown how considerably the bath–gymnasium complex is the product of Asia Minor alone.[14]

Baths on a block arrangement may have their origin in a fusion of the type of bath represented by the examples at Pompeii with the type of baths on compact rectangular or square plans found in rich villas of Campania.[15] Precise parallels for bath buildings with rectangular galleries are not found outside eastern Pamphylia or Rough Cilicia. Comparable rectangular galleries are to be seen in two baths, one of which is not too far from Pamphylia, the baths in the Sanctuary of Apollo Hylates at Curium in Cyprus (second century A.D.), and the baths of Trajanic and Hadrianic times in Cyrene (fig. 19).[16] In both these baths, a long gallery with a square basin at one end is set at one side of the main cluster of rooms. However, the long gallery communicates with all the first row of rooms on both sides of the gallery. The architects of these baths obviously intended to give the bather a choice of rooms to enter from this apodyterium/frigidarium, rather than insist that he follow a strict circulatory pattern from apodyteria through the usual sequence of heated rooms. It is the combination of these two features, the long gallery giving access to several different rooms at once, and the rectangular pool at the end of the long gallery, which suggests that the architects of this secluded corner of Asia Minor may have taken this

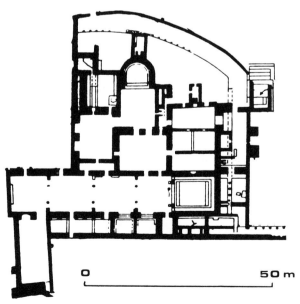

0   50 m

FIG. 19. Plan of the Baths of Trajan and Hadrian at Cyrene (after Crema, *op. cit.* (note 16), 415, by courtesy of Societa Editrice Internazionale)

motif from Cyprus or Cyrenaica, and increased its importance as a circulatory centre. The resulting rectangular plan also suggests the influences of plans on a block arrangement.

The reason for this unique plan was presumably the demands of the bathers of that part of Asia Minor. That bathing patterns may have differed here from the usual sequential pattern is suggested by the presence of individual basins, reminiscent of the individual basins of Hellenistic baths, in one room of the Baths II.7.a at Anemourium. Perhaps the bathers of this secluded area required the facilities for both old and new ways of bathing. This group of baths is anyway the creation of local architects in an area usually considered lacking in architectural traditions.[17]

Despite the diversity of bath design, the varieties of plans are quite strictly geographically limited, suggesting little cross-influence from region to region. Nevertheless, Asia Minor was an architecturally fertile place. Many substantial buildings fall outside the boundaries of our four categories. The architects of the western coastlands produce their own highly original version of the thermae of Rome, whilst a secluded corner of Pamphylia and Rough Cilicia produced its own unique plan.

NOTES

[1] J. B. Ward-Perkins, *Roman Imperial Architecture* (Harmondsworth, 1981), 273.

[2] F. K. Yeğül, 'The Bath–Gymnasium Complex in Asia Minor during the Imperial Age', Ph.D. thesis, Harvard University, 1975, 77–210.

[3] Sardis, Gymnasium: Yeğül, *op. cit.* (note 2), 98–105. Alexandria Troas, Gymnnasium: *ibid.*, 115–17: A. C. G. Smith in *AS*, xxix (1979), 23–50. Ephesus, East Gymnasium: e.g. Ward-Perkins, *op. cit.* (note 1), 293, fig. 190c; Theatre Gymnasium: e.g. J. Keil, *Ephesos: ein Führer durch die Ruinenstätte und ihre Geschichte*, 5th edn. (Vienna, 1964), 74–83; Gymnasium of Vedius: e.g. Ward-Perkins, *op. cit.* (note 1), 293, fig. 190b.

[4] F. K. Yeğül in *The Art Bulletin*, liv (1982), 7–31.

[5] Ephesus, Harbour Baths: e.g. Ward-Perkins, *op. cit.* (note 1), 293, fig. 190a. Hierapolis, 'Terme Extra Muros': P. Verzone in *Cahiers archéologiques*, viii (1956), 37–61. Laodicea ad Lycum, 'Gymnasium of Hadrian': G. Weber in *JDAI*, xix (1904), 95–6; G. E. Bean, *Turkey beyond the Maeander*, 2nd edn. (London, 1980), 217. Aphrodisias, 'Baths of Hadrian': *Comptes rendus de l'Académie des Inscriptions et Belles Lettres*, 1906, 158–84, and 1914, 46–53; K. Erim in *TAD*, xv.1 (1966), 63; xv.2 (1966), 58–9; xvi.1 (1967), 67–79. Aezani, Gymnasium: D. Krencker and E. Krüger, *Die Trierer Kaiserthermen* (Augsburg, 1929), 295; Yeğül, *op. cit.* (note 2), 131; R. Naumann in *AA*, 1980, 123–36, and 1983, 345–56. Ankara, Baths of Caracalla: Yeğül, *op. cit.* (note 2), 117–20; Ward-Perkins, *op. cit.* (note 1), 280, 292.

[6] 'Row-type' baths: E. Pfretzschner, *Die Grundrissentwicklung der roemischen Thermen* (Strasburg, 1909), *passim*. Anemourium, Baths II.11.b: E. Rosenbaum, G. Huber and S. Onurkan, *A Survey of Coastal Cities in Western Cilicia* (Ankara, 1967), 9–11; Baths and Palaestra III.2.b: e.g. Ward-Perkins, *op. cit.* (note 1), 304–5, fig. 199; Baths III.15: J. Russell in *TAD*, xxii.2 (1975); xxiv.2 (1977), 138; xxvii.2 (1980), 266–7. Antiochia ad Cragum, Baths I.12.a: Rosenbaum *et al.*, *op. cit.* (this note), 26–7, fig. 21; J. Russell in *TAD*, xxii.2 (1975), 55–71. Iotape, Baths 5b: Rosenbaum and Huber, *op. cit.* (this note), 39–40, figs. 26, 27, 29, pl. XVII, 2; Baths 6: *ibid.*, 36, 41–2, fig. 26, 94. Syedra, Baths II.1.a: *ibid.*, 45–6, fig. 32. Laodicea ad Lycum, North Baths: for this, and Perge, South Gymnasium (this note), Tripolis, Great Baths (this note), Perge, North Baths (below, note 8), Simena, Baths of Titus (below, note 8), Seleucia in Pamphylia, Baths (below, note 9), see A. Farrington, 'Imperial Bath Buildings in Lycia' (forthcoming). Perge, South Gymnasium: K. Lanckoronski, *Städte Pamphyliens und Pisidiens*, i: *Pamphylien* (Vienna, 1890), 39–40, fig. 20; G. E. Bean, *Turkey's Southern Shore*, 2nd edn. (London, 1979), 34; J. Inan in *Belleten Türk Tarih Kurumu*, xlv.2.179 (1981), 364–9; xlvi.184 (1982 [1983]), 973–8; Farrington, *op. cit.* (this note). Sillyum, Baths: Lanckoronski, *op. cit.* (this note), 64, 84, fig. 67.

[7] Grid plans in Roman baths: Pfretzschner, *op. cit.* (note 6), 25–8.

[8] Perge, North Baths: Lanckoronski, *op. cit.* (note 6), 41–4; J. B. Ward-Perkins in D. Talbot Rice (ed.), *The Great Palace of the Byzantine Emperors*, ii (Edinburgh, 1958), 52–104, at 101; Bean, *op. cit.* (note 6), 34–5; Farrington, *op. cit.* (note 6). Selge, 'Stadionthermen': A. Machatshek and M. Schwarz, *Bauforschungen in Selge* (Vienna, 1981), 82–4, pl. xi. Miletus, Baths of Capito: Ward-Perkins, *op. cit.* (this note), 99; G. Kleiner, *Die Ruinen von Milet* (Berlin, 1968), 91–2. Simena, Baths of Titus: C. Texier, *Description de l'Asie Mineure*, iii (Paris, 1849), 233–4; *IGR*, iii (1906), no. 690; G. E. Bean, *Lycian Turkey* (London, 1978), 117; Farrington, *op. cit.* (note 6). Corasium, Late Baths: *ibid*.

[9] Baths with central rectangular gallery: Anemourium, Baths II.7.a: Rosenbaum *et al.*, *op. cit.* (note 6), 5, fig. 4; L. C. Smith in *TAD*, xvii.2 (1968), 177–9; xviii.2 (1969), 47–58. Antiochia ad Cragum, Baths I.12.a: Rosenbaum *et al.*, *op. cit.* (note 6), 26–7, fig. 21; J. Russell in *TAD*, xxii.2 (1975), 55–71. Seleucia in Pamphylia, Baths: Bean, *op. cit.* (note 6), 88; Farrington, *op. cit.* (note 6). Syedra, Baths II.1.a: Rosenbaum *et al.*, *op. cit.* (note 6), 45–6, fig. 32; Farrington, *op. cit.* (note 6).

[10] Colophon, Baths: L. B. Holland in *Hesperia*, xiii (1944), 169, pl. x. Hellenistic baths at Hippocome in Lycia: E. Kalinka, *TAM*, ii (1920), no. 168.

[11] Hellenistic baths in general: R. Ginouvès, *Balaneutikè* (Paris, 1962), 183–224. Greek terms used for rooms in Imperial baths: Galen, *De Methodo Medendi*, 10.722, 723; *De Simplicium Medicamentorum Temperamentis ac Facultatibus*, 12.239.

[12] Pompeian baths, Stabian Baths: e.g. E. La Rocca, M. and A. de Vos and F. Coarelli, *Guida archeologica di Pompei*, 2nd edn. (1981), 296; Forum Baths: e.g. *ibid*., 131–6; Central Baths: *ibid*., 307–10. This type in Italy: R. Staccioli in *Classical Archaeology*, x (1958), 273 ff. Use of this type in the northern part of the Empire: Ward-Perkins, *op. cit.* (note 1), 217–18. 233–4, 478 n. 20.

[13] Thermae in Rome: e.g. Ward-Perkins, *op. cit.* (note 1), *passim*.

[14] Baths at Caunus: at present undergoing excavation by Professor B. Öğün, Ankara University. Baths at Timgad, Carthage, Cuicul, Trier: Ward-Perkins, *op. cit.* (note 1), 397–9, figs. 265(b)–7, 301–2. Bath–gymnasium complex as product of Asia Minor: Yeğül, *op. cit.* (note 2), 120–201.

[15] Baths in Campanian villas: E. Fabbricotti in *Cronache pompeiane*, ii (1976), 29–111.

[16] Baths in sanctuary of Apollo Hylates at Curium: e.g. V. Karagheorgis, *Cyprus from the Stone Age to the Romans* (London, 1982), 184–5, fig. 135. Trajanic and Hadrianic baths at Cyrene: e.g. L. Crema, *Enciclopedia classica* (1959), iii.12.1, 412–13, fig. 507.

[17] Ward-Perkins, *op. cit.* (note 1), 304–5.

Roman Nymphaea in the Greek World

Susan Walker, F.S.A.

The construction of Roman nymphaea at three major Achaean sites is here briefly considered. There follows a short discussion of the implications of this development for the production of architectural and sculptural decoration used in nymphaea and kindred buildings, of the nature of the Roman nymphaeum and of its usefulness to archaeologists and historians as an indicator of prosperity.

Many of the comments made here are drawn from observations made by the author in an unpublished doctoral thesis, 'The Architectural Development of Roman Nymphaea in Greece' (London, 1979).

The Nymphaeum of Herodes Atticus at Olympia

One of the more diverting of the peripatetic philosophers of second-century Greece was the Cynic Peregrinus Proteus of Parium on the Hellespont. Excommunicated by the Christians for allegedly profaning the rite of the Lord's Supper, he succeeded in obtaining a substantial following by publicly announcing his forthcoming suicide by self-immolation. His disciples grew in number after Peregrinus fulfilled his promise at the Olympic Games of A.D. 165.[1]

On an earlier visit to the sanctuary the philosopher had criticized the nymphaeum given by the millionaire Tiberius Claudius Atticus Herodes of Marathon, also a philosopher.[2] Such an amenity, Peregrinus claimed, made the Greeks effeminate. Amidst heroic contests of strength and grace the spectators should endure their thirst (Lucian, *Peregrinus*, 19). The criticism caused outrage and was later publicly withdrawn.[3] The satirist Lucian of Samosata, warming to his theme of the ludicrous antics of the attention-seeking Peregrinus, offered some arguments in defence of Herodes' nymphaeum (*idem*). Peregrinus, he scoffed, was a hypocrite, for he had actually dared to attack the building while drinking its waters. And these were of undeniable benefit to the hordes of visitors to the sanctuary. In the days before the construction of the nymphaeum, pilgrims had been succumbing in their thousands, victims of infections, poisoned by bad wells.

Even at a distance of nearly two millennia, both sides of this argument may be clearly appreciated. Herodes' fresh-water fountain may well have saved lives and unquestionably provided much-needed refreshment for the huge throng of people then visiting the sanctuary. But it was a monster, much more so than Schleif and Weber's published reconstructions of 1944 would have us believe.[4] Recent work on the nymphaeum has shown beyond reasonable doubt that the buttressed apsidal wall of the upper basin supported two stories of statues, most of them portraits of Herodes and the reigning emperor Antoninus Pius and their families, arranged in such a way as to suggest, even to the unlettered, a significant relationship.[5]

The nymphaeum towered over the ancient Temple of Hera, its crude gaudy statues and coloured marble revetment blanching the little treasuries on the terrace to the east.[6] In effect the fountain became, like the Library in which Tiberius Celsus Polemaeanus had recently been buried at Ephesus, a dynastic monument.[7] Statues were updated. Thus Marcus Aurelius, a young man at the time of the nymphaeum's construction in about A.D. 150, was portrayed in later life as sole emperor, his cuirassed statue set in a rotunda inserted at one end of the lower basin; a togate statue, probably representing the elderly Herodes, was set in a similar structure at the other end. These were probably dedicated in the 170s, perhaps to commemorate the reconciliation of Herodes with the Athenians, following the personal intervention of the emperor, whom Herodes had once instructed in philosophy. Later Herodes' son-in-law Vibullius Hipparchus revised the outdated texts of some of the bases of the statues set around the upper basin, and added new statues of members of his own family to commemorate his improvements to the aqueduct.[8]

The most recent reconstruction of the nymphaeum by Renate Bol includes two representations of Zeus, patron god of the river Alphaeus, whose waters had been captured for the fountain.[9] On the wall between upper and lower basin stood a marble bull with its flank inscribed 'Regilla, priestess of Demeter, [gave] the water and the [images] around the water to Zeus' (pl. V*a*).[10] The language, elliptical and archaizing in the fashion of Greek *litterati* of the day, was intended to recall a primitive sacrifice, such as had been made, according to the contemporary traveller Pausanias (i.14.1), by the Archaic tyrant Theagenes to the river-god Achelous, whose waters he had captured to feed the people of Megara.

Theagenes built his altar not in Megara, but up in the hills at Rhous, at the spot where the waters had been diverted. But no visitor to Olympia was likely to trek up the Miraka valley to marvel at the piety of Herodes and his wife Regilla, who elsewhere in the Altis dedicated a statue to Hygieia, perhaps in reflection of the beneficial effect of the nymphaeum.[11] The act of sacrifice was transported to the terminus of the aqueduct for everyone to see, and even today we may admire the bull, immortalized in stone, in the new museum.

This nymphaeum is a very sophisticated building, rich in allusion, expressive of the relationship between the local community of the Eleans, who gave the statues of Herodes and his family, and the wealthiest family of Antonine Greece, and between Herodes, who gave the imperial portraits, and the rulers of the day. It reeks, too, of nostalgia for a simpler past. To build it Herodes employed the most up-to-date technology and construction techniques (see below). If such a building were to be constructed today, it would no doubt cause much comment as an outrageous triumph of post-modernism. To the intellectual peers of Lucian and Peregrinus it may well have carried some of the associations that such a term implies.

Greece had not long been in a position to expect such gifts from her magnates. It was imperial interest on the part of Hadrian that had made the place so fashionable. More than one ancient writer repeatedly claimed that Hadrian had pulled Greece from a miasma of neglect, a view that derives some support from the archaeological evidence for a remarkable increase in public building in Achaea under Hadrian and the Antonines, and from the epigraphic evidence for the increased numbers of visitors to the major cities and sanctuaries, numbers of important foreigners holding religious or public office, intermarriage between Achaeans and foreign notables, and so on.[12]

It was Greece's distinguished past that attracted Hadrian and his followers, as it has attracted the romantic traveller in more recent times. But Hadrian, 'the little Greek', as his Roman detractors called him, may also have had more rational motives in favouring old Greece. To make impoverished Athens the centre of the Greek-speaking world, as he effectively did, put the competitive over-spenders of Asia in their proper place.

Contemporary development of Athens and its water supply

Hadrian furnished Athens as the capital city of the Greek world, prefiguring the role later given to Byzantium. Athens was the only provincial city in the empire to receive annually a guaranteed supply of corn. Masons and sculptors were put to work on a grandiose programme of public buildings of high quality; the most spectacular of these was the Temple of Olympian Zeus, dedicated on an imperial visit made in A.D. 131–2. The temple had been started some seven hundred years previously by the Athenian tyrant Pisistratus. Another project of Pisistratus had been a water supply from the Ilissus valley to the Agora in the centre of the city. As with the temple, seven hundred years were to pass before Hadrian had a new external aqueduct constructed. An underground tunnel led from the sources on Mount Parnes to Mount Lycabettus, where, high above the city, reservoirs were fronted by an elegant Ionic portico, drawn in the eighteenth century by James 'Athenian' Stuart and Nicholas Revett.[13] The entablature bore a Latin inscription recording the completion of the aqueduct by Hadrian's successor Antoninus Pius in the year of his third consulate, A.D. 140 (pl. V*b*).[14]

Under Pius, who never visited Greece, it again became the duty, as it has remained for much of recorded history, of the rich to provide for the communities from which they derived their wealth. Buildings of public utility were an important element in such endowments. The burden of obligation to make such provisions was mitigated by the glory that rebounded upon the family of the donor, whose members were immortalized in marble statues and whose virtue was permanently recorded in the dedicatory inscription upon the building and in honours granted by the grateful community.[15]

In terms of providing a showcase for such rewards, the nymphaeum of Herodes, used by thousands of visitors to Olympia, must be judged a prime site (fig. 20, top). A nymphaeum resembling that of Herodes in its plan, decoration, and the undeniably second-rate quality of its statuary was constructed at the highest point in the Athenian Agora.[16] Only fragments survive, for the structure was deliberately demolished in the aftermath of the Herulian raids on the city in A.D. 267. The fountain appears to be the

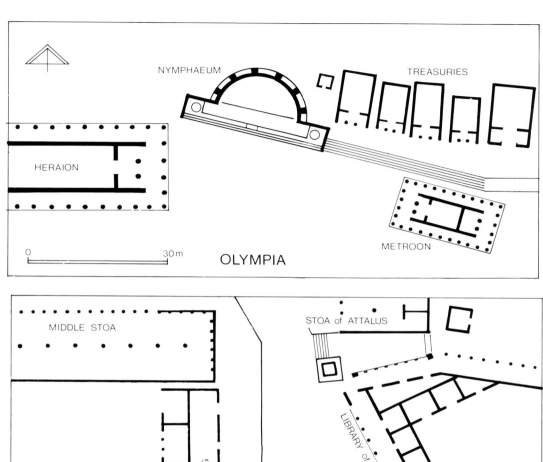

Fig. 20. Top, site plan of the nymphaeum of Herodes Atticus at Olympia; bottom, site plan of the nymphaeum in the Athenian Agora

terminus of an extension to Hadrian's aqueduct. Like the nymphaeum at Olympia, it was deliberately contrived to catch the attention of passers-by (fig. 20). An earlier Roman fountain nearby had closed off the south end of the terrace of the East Building, but the Antonine nymphaeum was swivelled to look into that great processional route, the Panathenaic Way. Spectators of the festival could shelter from the elements in a stoa opposite the nymphaeum, built at about the same time. A statue was placed in the centre of the terrace fronting the basin. Its axis, and that of the fountain, might be produced to glance off the south-west corner of the Stoa of Attalus, a clever plan that offered an impressive vista to the visitor arriving in the Agora through the arch ending the pedestrian street linking the so-called Roman Agora with the ancient centre of Athenian public life (fig. 20, bottom).[17]

The water-supply of Argos in the second century A.D.

A situation similar to that of Athens obtained in the Dorian mother-city of Argos, notorious for its lack of water. Here, too, Hadrian paid for a lengthy aqueduct terminating in a porticoed reservoir high above the city.[18] The vaulted building, much better preserved than its Athenian counterpart (which, with the aqueduct, was revamped to cater for the rapid expansion of the Europeanized capital city in the later nineteenth century), was contrived to resemble a grotto (pl. VI*a*).[19] Hadrian, heroic in stature, naked and holding his sword, stood poised over the water outlet (pl. VI*b*). The lower walls of the reservoir were cut from rock; the upper walls and the vault were of brick and concrete. The water cascaded over marble steps. Here, as at Olympia, the upper basin served to cleanse the water of limey deposits. And, as on the slopes of Lycabettus, the fake grotto was fronted by an Ionic portico. Also reminiscent of Athens is the later extension of water-works to the Argive Agora. Of particular interest is an inscription rebuilt into the stylobate of a late Roman palaestra in the baths to the south of the Agora. It refers to a prominent Argive family, known from other inscriptions, one member of whom is said, in that arch Antonine language familiar to connoisseurs of Herodes' work at Olympia, to have 'brought the waters down from above'.[20]

Despite recent careful excavation of the Agora at Argos, our understanding of the functions of the two nymphaea thus far found there remains elusive. One, a circular structure equipped with underground passage and surrounded by a colonnade, is inscribed (I reconstruct the missing first three words) '[the aqueduct with] the springs and the nymphaeum with the reservoir' (pl. VII*a*). This may be a reference to the Hadrianic aqueduct and the works on the Larissa hill (above). The rotunda is not aligned with other structures in the Agora and the underground passage leads north. The structure is dated by numismatic evidence to the end of Hadrian's reign.[21] A square fountain, apparently surmounted by a miniature *quadrifrons*, was constructed some sixty years later about 40 m. to the west. This, the gift of the Tiberii Julii family, is similarly a functional puzzle (pl. VII*b*).[22]

The circular building at Argos is unusual in bearing an inscription with a specific reference to a nymphaeum.[23] 'Functional' fountains were called by the Greeks χρῆναι, and by the Romans *munera* (public works of obligation), a term that firmly classes aqueducts and fountains with libraries, theatres, city gates, gymnasia and baths, all of which might be decorated by their donors with self-advertising statues and eye-catching marble revetment. A nymphaeum, properly speaking, was a sanctu-

PLATE V

a. Olympia: the bull dedicated in the name of Regilla

b. Athens, Zappeion Gardens: part of the inscribed entablature of the portico of Hadrian's aqueduct

PLATE VI

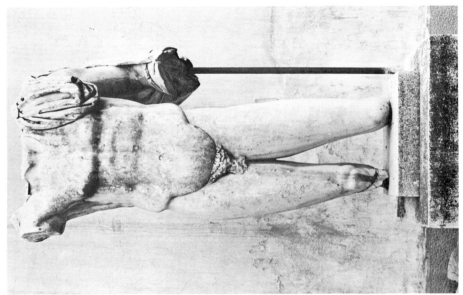

Argos

a. The Hadrianic nymphaeum on the slopes of Larissa

b. The statue of Hadrian from the nymphaeum

PLATE VII

a. The rotunda in the Agora

b. The 'monument carré' in the Agora

Argos

ary in which the nymphs were worshipped, a classical notion as far removed from 'the new city of Hadrian' (as Athens was now called), as from the crowded sanctuaries of Olympia, Epidaurus and Delphi. But while parts of Greece had become developed, other sites survived, as Pausanias noted, where magical springs cured even such maladies as the melancholia of unrequited love (vii.23.2). There is, he noted with scorn, a city in Phocis where they have 'no state buildings at all, no training-grounds, no theatre and no market-square, no running water at a water-head and they live on the edge of a torrent in hovels like mountain huts'. 'Still', he sniffed, 'their territory has boundary stones with its neighbours and they send delegates to the Phocian assembly' (x.4.1). Alongside the Roman nymphaea, with all their protestations of nostalgia and the self-advancement of the virtuous aristocracy, the nymphs and more shadowy deities had their place, especially where the credulous sought a cure for disease or guidance upon their future.

Materials and methods of production

The drive to supply growing communities with fountains properly described as *munera* was partially responsible for the generation of sophisticated methods of construction in which components were supplied to similarly decorated public (and, we may assume, though archaeological evidence is lacking, to private) buildings. Athens had supported workshops of craftsmen producing Pentelic marble column capitals and bases at least since the days of Augustus.[24] When there was insufficient work in Athens, as was apparently the case for much of the first century A.D., they travelled elsewhere.[25] Some of their work may be seen in the first-century buildings at Corinth and, for example, in the first phase of the buildings now known as 'Thermes du Théâtre' at Argos.[26] Here the capitals were apparently used with greyish unfluted monolithic columns, possibly of Hymettan marble. By Hadrian's time, the fashion had turned to the mixing of white Pentelic with green Cipollino columns from Euboea, used to great effect in the west façade of the Library at Athens,[27] The same mixture appears in the late Hadrianic rotunda at Argos, in an extension and apparent transformation of role, contemporary with the rotunda, of the Thermes du Théâtre, and in the later Antonine monopteroi of Herodes' nymphaeum at Olympia.[28] Nor was the scope of Athenian craftsmen limited to the province of Achaea. The same combination of marbles turns up in the Forum Baths at Ostia, dedicated in A.D. 160, with capitals remarkably like those of the monopteroi at Olympia.[29] And when the commissions in Greece began to run thin under the Severi, and Greece lost its central position within the empire to the cities of Africa, Athenian craftsmen were to be found at work on the great Forum of the emperor's native city, Lepcis Magna.[30]

The increase in scale and scope of the construction of public buildings in the Aegean provinces and areas with which they had contact may account for the growth of standardization in architectural and figured decoration. Cipollino column shafts were evidently cut as monoliths to a standard length in the quarries on Euboea. Pentelic capitals and bases were, in another quarry, cut to fit the heights and diameters of the column shafts. In some cases the entablatures appear to have been made of another marble.

Another Pentelic workshop was engaged in the production of large numbers of statues. Bodies were conventionalized into the quaintly named forms that have come down to us from earlier generations of classifiers: *grosse und kleine Herkulänerin*, and so forth. More attention was paid to the heads, often cut from separate blocks of stone of higher quality, and endowed with sufficient characterization of the individual portrayed to allow some degree of recognition to those who could not or did not read the accompanying texts. Nobody bothered much with the backs, since these figures were destined to be packed into the walls of the buildings, framed by projecting marble orders and protected by canopies. Even the fronts might be left fairly rough, for they would be placed far above eye level.[31]

On site, the architect and builders must have planned for the arrival of these components from various sources. At Olympia even the bricks may have been imported. They were stamped with the name of the donor of the nymphaeum, a rare practice in Roman Greece, where most bricks appear to have been produced for immediate local use, and there was hence no need to advertise their origin and quality.[32] There is some evidence to suggest that the designer of the nymphaeum worked to a perfect mathematical system, a numerical progression of multiples of 3 Roman feet, the thickness of the walls.[33]

Conclusion

In the major cities and sanctuaries of Hadrianic and Antonine Greece we may find evidence of knowledge of hydraulic technology, of sophisticated forms of building, and an acute awareness of the messages that might be conveyed to grateful or to cynical users by a building's form and decoration. Donors of nymphaea might be imperial, notables of local origin, or even foreigners attracted by the prestige of improving provision for water in a venerable old province. Among the latter we may count the senator Sextus Julius Maior Antoninus Pythodorus of Nysa in Caria, who sponsored various projects at Epidaurus, among them a fresh water supply for the doubtless increased numbers of visitors to the healing sanctuary of Asclepius;[34] and at Corinth, the celebrated old Fountain of Peirene was decorated in marble and kitted out with a statue of the eponymous nymph and marble-plated exedrae where old men could sit to admire the water-carriers, as they had done in the days of Euripides. The unknown donor of the exedrae (not, as has commonly been supposed, the ubiquitous Herodes), recorded his good works in Latin.[35] Surviving archaeological, literary and epigraphic evidence offers an outline of the workings of a complex system, in which nymphaea (in the modern usage of the term, borrowed from later antiquity) might be counted an index of prosperity. The Roman nymphaeum only became widespread in old Greece when the province of Achaea became the focus of imperial interest. The building of large fountains supplied by lengthy aqueducts presupposes sufficient money, expertise, effective control over the territory in question, the ability to maintain a complex system, and a population, whether resident or visiting, of a size to merit the investment.[36] In other Greek-speaking provinces, notably Asia, these conditions existed in the first century A.D., and we find nymphaea even more elaborate than that of Herodes impressing the residents of, say, Miletus or Ephesus as early as the reign of Titus.[37] Small wonder that, on both shores of the Aegean, substantial cracks in the urban super- and infrastructure developed in the chaotic years of the third century, and the proconsuls and correctors of the Tetrarchy and later years had much to do in the way of restoration.[38]

We do well to remember the impression of second-century Achaea given by Pausanias: prosperity existed in pockets, with wasted depopulated land between them, where the few surviving residents clambered down to rivers for their water, or were fortunate enough to possess a good spring blessed by the likes of Bellerophon and watched over by a kindly nymph.

Acknowledgements

Figure 20 was drawn by Susan Bird, after plans published by W. Dörpfeld, A. Mallwitz and H. A. Thompson. Plate VI*a* was photographed by Alan S. Walker; the other photographs were taken by the author in the course of research for a doctoral thesis on Roman nymphaea in Greece (1974-6). Among the many friends and colleagues who helped and advised with this project, the author would like to thank Dr H. W. Catling, Dr R. Bol, Professor H. A. Thompson, Professor R. Ginouvès, Dr P. Aupert, Dr P. Marchetti and Dr E. Romiopoulou.

NOTES

[1] Lucian, *Peregrinus*; Philostratus, *Vitae Sophistorum*, ii.1.563. See also G. Bowersock, *Greek Sophists in the Roman Empire* (Oxford, 1969),3; C. Robinson, *Lucian* (London, 1979), 58; W. Ameling, *Herodes Atticus* (Hildesheim, 1983), i, 93–4.

[2] See most recently R. Bol, *Olympische Forschungen*, xv: *Das Statuenprogramm des Herodes-Atticus-Nymphäums* (Berlin, 1984).

[3] Lucian, *Peregrinus*, 20. S. Settis, 'Il ninfeo di Erode Attico a Olympia e il problema della composizione della Periegesi di Pausania', *Ann. Pisa*, ser. 2, xxxvii (1968), esp. 17–24.

[4] H. Schleif and H. Weber, *Olympische Forschungen*, i (1944), Taf. 36–7.

[5] Bol, *op. cit.* (note 2), Beilage 4–5.

[6] Adjacent buildings are illustrated in the reconstructed section and elevation by Schleif and Weber, *op. cit.* (note 4).

[7] On the Library of Celsus, see V. M. Strocka, 'Zur Datierung der Celsus-Bibliothek', *Proceedings of the Xth International Congress of Classical Archaeology, Ankara-Izmir, 1973* (Ankara, 1978), 893–900.

[8] Bol, *op. cit.* (note 2), 157, no. 30, for the original version of Marcus Aurelius; 101 and 193–5, nos. 50–1 for the figures in the monopteroi; 139–40 for alterations made by Vibullius Hipparchus.

[9] Bol, *op. cit.* (note 2), 187–93, nos. 48–9.

[10] Bol, *op. cit.* (note 2), 109, Bau- und Weihinschriften no. 1, with refs. n. 366.

[11] *Olympia*, v (1896), no. 288. See Bol, *op. cit.* (note 2), 109, n. 366. On the aqueduct, see A. von Gerkan, *Olympiabericht*, i (1937), 16 ff., and A. Mallwitz, *Olympia und seine Bauten* (Munich, 1972), 149–55.

[12] On the cultural and architectural development of Achaea under Hadrian and the Antonines, see A. Spawforth and S. Walker, 'The world of the Panhellenion. I: Athens and Eleusis', *JRS*, lxxv (1985), 78–104, and 'II: Three Dorian Cities', *JRS*, lxxvi (1986), 88–105.

[13] J. Stuart and N. Revett, *Antiquities of Athens*, iii (1794), ch. 4. See also J. Travlos, *A Pictorial Dictionary of Ancient Athens* (New York, 1971), 242–3.

[14] *CIL*, iii, 549.

[15] For an account of this practice in the Imperial period in Italy, see B. Ward-Perkins, *From Classical Antiquity to the Middle Ages* (Oxford, 1984), 3–13.

[16] H. A. Thompson, *The Athenian Agora*, 3rd edn. (Athens, 6976), 151–2, with references to earlier publications, p. 317. For the pilaster capitals from the nymphaeum, see S. Walker in *AA*, 1979, 117–19.

[17] For a detailed account of the development of this area in the Roman period, see T. Leslie Shear, Jr., 'Athens: from city-state to provincial town', *Hesperia*, l (1981), 356–77, and Spawforth and Walker, *op. cit.* (note 12).

[18] For the aqueduct, see W. Vollgraff in *BCH*, xliv (1920), 224, and P. Aupert in *BCH*, cvii (1983), 849–50. For the nymphaeum, Vollgraff in *BCH*, lxxxii (1958), 516 ff. The inscriptions were published by Vollgraff in *BCH*, lxviii–lxix (1946), 397–400. A new survey of the building is promised: *BCH*, cvi (1982), 644.

[19] Vollgraff, *op. cit.* (note 18: 1958), and R. Ginouvès, *Laodicée du Lykos: le nymphée* (Quebec, 1969), 141, and *L'Odéon d'Argos et le théâtron à gradins droits* (Paris, 1972), 217–45: appendix: 'L'appareil en briques'. Compare the portrait of Hadrian (Vollgraff, *op. cit.*, note 18 (1958)) with statues found at Pergamum and Vaison-la-Romaine: M. Wegner, *Das Bildnis des Kaisers Hadrians* (Berlin, 1956), 105, 115–16, Tafel 14b.

[20] *BCH*, cii (1978), 784, E92; 782, fig. 19.

[21] *BCH*, xcix (1975), 703; c (1976), 753; ci (1977), 672–3. For an account of earlier excavations, see *BCH*, lxxviii (1954), 160 ff.; lxxxi (1957), 663 ff. For the coin, see *BCH*, cii (1978), 798.

[22] *BCH*, xcix (1975), 703; c (1976), 753; ci (1977), 672–3. For the relationship of this structure to the extension of the classical portico to the south, see M. Pierart and J.-P. Thalmann, *Études Argiennes*, BCH Suppl. (1980), 459.

[23] The best discussion of the term 'nymphaeum' is by S. Settis, 'Esedra e ninfeo nella terminologia architettonica del mondo Romano dall'età republicana alla tarda antichità', *ANRW*, i.4 (1973), 661–745.

[24] J. Day, *An Economic History of Athens under Roman Domination* (New York, 1942), 204–7.

[25] Walker, *op. cit.* (note 16), 103–29.

[26] For a general account of the urban development of Corinth, see J. Wiseman, *ANRW*, ii.7.1 (1979), 509–43. Full publication of the Thermes du Théâtre at Argos is in progress; for recent work on the baths, see the relevant entries in 'Rapports sur les travaux de l'École Française en Grèce', in the following numbers of *BCH*: xcviii (1974); c (1976); cv (1981) and cvi (1982).

[27] Travlos, *op. cit.* (note 13), 248, fig. 319.

[28] I am grateful to P. Aupert and P. Marchetti for allowing me to see unpublished capitals from Argos. Monolithic columns are preserved on both sites. For the capitals from Olympia, see Schleif and Weber, *op. cit.* (note 4), 81, Abb. 21, and W.-D. Heilmeyer, *Korinthische Normalkapitelle*, Röm-Mitt, Ergänzungsheft 16 (1970), 76 ff., 100, 104, 107, Taf. 31, 1–2.

[29] Heilmeyer, *op. cit.* (note 28), Taf. 31, 3–4. P. Pensabene, *Scavi di Ostia*, vii.1: *I Capitelli* (1972), no. 333.

[30] J. B. Ward-Perkins, 'Tripolitania and the marble trade', *JRS*, xli (1951), 89–104. See also J. M. Reynolds and J. B. Ward-Perkins, *Inscriptions of Roman Tripolitania* (London, 1952), 190–192, nos. 799–804.

[31] On the quality of Antonine sculptures at Olympia and Athens, see Bol, *op. cit.* (note 2), 20–1, and E. Harrison, *The Athenian Agora*, i: *Portrait Sculpture* (Princeton, 1953), 44, no. 33.

[32] F. Adler, *Olympia Ergebnisse*, ii (1892), 135. See also R. Ginouvès, *op. cit.* (note 19), 145–6 and 220.

[33] This point was raised in the author's thesis (see note above, p. 60), pp. 185–6, fig. 61, but no published confirmation has resulted from recent surveys of the site.

[34] On Sextus Julius Maior, see H. Halfmann, *Die Senatoren aus dem östlichen Teil des Imperium Romanum bis zum Ende des 2 Jhr.n.Chr.* (Göttingen, 1979), 171–2, no. 89, with other refs. p. 225.

[35] J. H. Kent, *Corinth*, viii.3: *Greek and Latin Inscriptions* (Cambridge, Mass., 1966), no. 135. See also J. Wiseman, *op. cit.* (note 26), 526 and n. 347.

[36] P. Leveau and J.-L. Paillet, *L'Alimentation en eau de Caesarea de Mauretanie et l'aqueduc de Cherchell* (Paris, 1976), 15–20; B. Shaw, 'Water and society in the ancient Maghrib: technology, property and development', *Antiquités africaines*, xx (1984), 121–73.

[37] On the date of the so-called Nymphaeum of Trajan at Miletus, see B. Kreiler, *Die Statthalter Kleinasiens unter den Flaviern* (Munich, 1975), 34–38. For a later Flavian and a Trajanic nymphaeum at Ephesus, see F. Miltner, *JÖAI*, xlv (1960), Beibl., 27 ff., and xliv (1969), Beibl., 326 ff., and A. Bammer, *Architektur und Gesellschaft in der Antike* (Vienna, 1974), 124–7.

[38] A. H. M. Jones, *The Greek City from Alexander to Justinian*, 2nd edn. (Oxford, 1966), 147 ff.

Roman Aqueducts in Asia Minor

J. J. Coulton, F.S.A.

In the early second century A.D. the brilliant administrator Frontinus ended the introductory section of his account of the water-supply system of Rome with these words, addressed to the emperor Trajan: 'You may compare the massive size and value of these many aqueducts with the unprofitable pyramids or those other useless but celebrated works of the Greeks.'[1] This contrast of the formal beauties of Greek architecture with the functional solidity of Roman engineering is a commonplace of many books on the Romans, and the image of aqueducts striding across the Roman Campagna is a powerful one which no Greek city before the time of Augustus could begin to match. It was not, of course, that the Greeks made no use of external water supplies. As early as the sixth century B.C. water piped from springs several kilometres away to the north-east was brought to a fountain on the Athenian Agora,[2] and at about the same time the tyrant Polycrates drove a spectacular tunnel beneath the acropolis hill of Samos to bring in water from a spring outside the city.[3] Three and a half centuries later the royal city of Pergamum was supplied by several pipelines of which the most ambitious consisted of three separate pipes running 30 km. from springs to the north and ending with a dramatic pressure section, descending 200 m. from the head tank, then rising 160 m. to reach the top of the citadel.[4]

But these are the exceptions. Most Greek cities before the Roman period relied on springs within, or close outside, the city walls, and on wells and cisterns. There is, therefore, a dramatic change to the situation in the early third century A.D., by which time most of the cities of the Greek east had built themselves external water supplies, often involving elaborate arched aqueducts and other major civil engineering works. At first sight this might look like a clear example of the Greeks imitating their rulers and adopting a characteristic Roman building type, just the kind of phenomenon that we are here considering.

But the truth is perhaps rather more complicated. It would have been more appropriate for Frontinus to compare the Roman aqueducts not with the beautiful, but useless, temples and so on, but with the almost unending series of fortifications which, in terms of sheer bulk, constituted for most Greek cities by far their greatest architectural undertaking, and which in the fragmented and insecure state of the Greek world were not just useful, but essential for survival. They remind us that the absence of earlier Greek parallels for the aqueducts of Rome was not due to poverty, ignorance, or inefficiency, but to the very obvious dangers of dependence on a visible and vulnerable lifeline from outside. So Greek water supplies from outside were virtually always underground pipelines without significant surface structures. How far they would actually be undetectable by an observant and determined enemy must remain uncertain, and in fact most cities also had cisterns and/or wells to depend on in an emergency, if the water line was found and cut. However, a cut pipeline could be much more easily repaired than the damage which could be inflicted on a high, built aqueduct.

The reality of the danger was shown later on at Rome itself. During their siege of the city in A.D. 537, the Goths not only cut off Rome's water supply by destroying the aqueducts, but also came near to entering the city unnoticed along the channel of the Aqua Virgo.[5]

The surprising thing is, therefore, not the slowness of the Greeks to build aqueducts, even though they certainly had the technical expertise to make such arched structures before 300 B.C. Rather it is the early date at which the Romans felt confident enough to build them. Rome's first two water-supply lines, the Appia and the Anio Vetus, built in 312 and 269 B.C., were, like the Greek ones, almost entirely underground, and did not enter Rome on a superstructure. But in 144 B.C., only two generations after Hannibal had thrown a spear over the walls of Rome, Q. Marcius Rex brought the Aqua Marcia over 90 km. from the upper Anio river, with the last 9 km. running on arches.[6] Clearly, there was considerable discussion about this at Rome. Frontinus simply tells of a dispute as to whether it was proper, in the face of a warning from the Sibylline books, to bring water to the Capitol.[7] But since it was the long, lofty, arched stretch which allowed the water to reach the Capitol, much of the argument must have turned on the question of whether such a high-level approach was appropriate. In the event, of course, Marcius Rex won the day, and his judgement was proved right by the lapse of about four hundred years before the city of Rome next felt the need for fortifications.

But in the second century B.C. this sense of security applied to few places outside Rome. The water supply of Aletrium in Latium, constructed around 100 B.C., involved not only a substantial siphon system across the Cosa valley, but also a high arched bridge across the river at the bottom.[8] But Ostia and Pompeii did not get long-distance water supplies before the time of Augustus,[9] and this was also the period of the next major aqueducts at Rome.[10] In the provinces, too, the great Pont du Gard, supplying Nîmes in Southern Gaul, is usually, although not certainly, dated to the same period,[11] and, on a much smaller scale, the aqueduct of Sextilius Pollio supplying Ephesus was built between A.D. 4 and 14 The latter is apparently the earliest of the built aqueducts of Asia Minor which are my main theme, and the mouldings and entablature, as well as the monumental inscription, on the arches which took it across the main road from Ephesus to Magnesia and the Maeander valley show that it was indeed meant to be seen.[12] The reign of Augustus, then, seems to be the time when, no doubt with some official encouragement, cities began to feel that the longed-for peace was sufficiently well established to justify the more or less elaborate water supplies, and the spread of such systems over the next two centuries to cities large and small all over the eastern empire is as much a response to the Pax Romana as a direct imitation of Rome.

It was, in fact, this connection between defence and water supply which particularly drew my attention to the water-supply system which has been the focus of my interest in the aqueducts of Asia Minor. Oenoanda is a small city in the mountains of south-west Asia Minor. It is best known for the long Epicurean inscription set up by a wealthy citizen called Diogenes, to which Professor Smith of Bangor has recently added many new fragments.[13] But since 1974 the British Institute at Ankara has, with the co-operation of the Turkish authorities, conducted a full survey of the surface remains of the city, architectural and epigraphic, under the direction of the late Mr Alan Hall of Keele University, to whom I owe my own participation in the project.[14]

Under the Roman Empire Oenoanda formed part of Lycia, but previously its relations with the Lycians were probably rather hostile, and its inhabitants had chosen a defensive site 300 m. above the surrounding upland plain. In addition, the weakest approaches, from the south and west, are strengthened by a well-built fortification wall which dates probably from the early second century B.C. The first plan of the site, published by Spratt and Forbes in 1847,[15] already showed an aqueduct crossing the saddle to the south of the city walls, and further investigation has shown that the conduit came from springs to the south, and along the intervening ridge, and then crossed the saddle in the direction of the south fortification wall in order to enter the city.[16] Quite close to the city wall there are several blocks visible of a stone pipeline, a feature to which I will return (fig. 21). But for the moment the question is whether the pipeline passed under or through the wall or whether the wall gave way to the pipeline. The slight diversion of the pipeline round the projecting pentagonal tower already implies that the tower is earlier, and when we look at the masonry of the fortification wall at the point where the line of the pipes would have met it, the original masonry appears to stop abruptly, presumably to let the pipeline through, so confirming the sequence: pipeline later than wall. Although certainty is impossible without excavation, it seems likely that with the passage of the pipeline the original fortifications had been given up. The untidy masonry which replaces the original work probably belongs with the late housing built against and over the line of the Hellenistic south wall, at a time when the defensive line of the city had been moved further north. But even if this masonry is an attempt to rebuild the fortification, such careless work would necessarily have left it seriously weakened, so that in either event there can be little doubt that water supply has taken precedence over defence. Similar values are embodied by the aqueduct, built perhaps in the second century A.D., which runs right up to the Hellenistic walls of Side in Pamphylia, for although the walls were not dismantled, the aqueduct would provide a lofty vantage point for any enemy and the water channel passed through the wall in a hole 0·46 by 0·42 m., quite big enough for a hostile intruder to slip through.[17] A comparable indication that walls were no longer felt to be necessary is provided by those cities, like Pergamum or, nearer at hand, Balbura and Limyra, which were now willing to spread outside the safety of their walls.[18] Just when the cities in various parts of Asia Minor felt it safe enough to prejudice their defences in these ways is a topic which deserves more investigation than there is space for here.[19]

In scale the Oenoanda water supply is rather meagre, with only a single pipeline running about 5 km. from the springs. In contrast, Side drew its water from springs about 30 km. away, with at least fifteen built aqueducts in its course,[20] and at

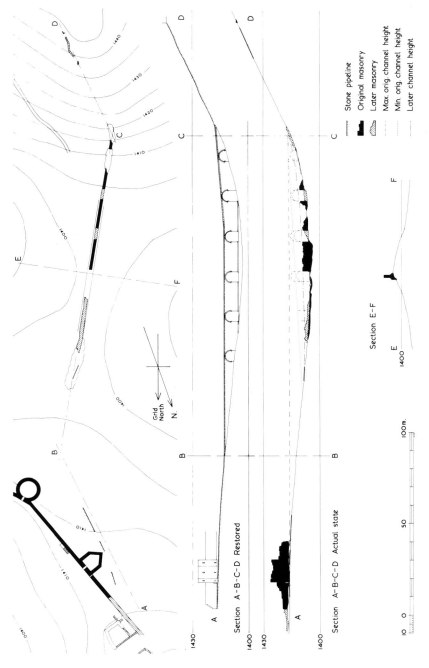

FIG. 21. Oenoanda (Lycia): the aqueduct, pipeline and Hellenistic south wall

Pergamum, whose water supply is now the best studied in Asia Minor, thanks to intensive work by the Leichtweiss-Institut für Wasserbau at Braunschweig, the Hellenistic pipelines were supplemented in the Roman period by three major supply channels, of which the longest ran 55 km. and required not one but some thirty-five separate aqueducts.[21] Even this length was far surpassed elsewhere, however. Given the dry North African climate, it is perhaps not surprising that the supply system of Carthage had to stretch 100 km. to find a satisfactory spring,[22] but so too did the water supply of Roman Cologne in the dampness of Germany.[23]

Length is, of course, not itself a virtue in a water-supply system, if adequate springs are near at hand, and in Asia Minor most cities were small enough to be satisfied without going too far afield. An extreme case was Phaselis in south-east Lycia, which drew its water from a spring only half a kilometre from the city centre, although an arched aqueduct was required for most of that distance.[24] Quantity is a more important factor and, with only a single pipe with a 14 cm. bore, the Oenoanda supply system would probably have provided about 1,000 m³. per day, whereas it has been calculated that Pergamum could dispose of 31,500 m³. per day.

Clay pipelines had been the normal water-carrier for earlier Greek water systems, and continued to be used in the Roman period, as at Ephesus. But under the Empire many Greek cities preferred a built channel, such as the Romans had used since the fourth century B.C. Such channels were typically 0·5–0·6 m. wide by 1·2–1·5 m. high, so that even though they would not be expected to run full,[25] they could obviously take the place of very many pipelines.

There is one situation, however, where pipes had a special role to play, and that is when the water crossed low ground by means of an inverted siphon. The high arched aqueducts of Rome and the Empire are such striking monuments that it is easy to suppose that Roman water courses were always given a continuous fall, achieved by bridging any valleys or low ground in the way. Certainly, this was normally the case, but the avoidance of siphons was a matter of greater convenience in construction and maintenance, not a matter of ignorance or inability;[26] so, too, arched structures were themselves avoided by detours, provided that the additional distance was not excessive. That the technology was already available is shown by the case of Pergamum, where the Hellenistic pipelines all used inverted siphons with the pipes under pressure to deliver the water into the hilltop city, and in the last and greatest of them, which served the acropolis itself, a 27 cm. lead pipeline rose, as we have seen, 160 m. from its lowest point, which gave it probably the greatest head of any siphon attempted in the ancient world.

The most impressive siphons of the Imperial period are those of southern Gaul, particularly those on the aqueducts serving Lyon, which have to cross a number of valleys, too deep to be bridged by an aqueduct maintaining the normal fall and too long for a detour round them to be practical.[27] At the Beaunant siphon on the Gier aqueduct the water descends *c.* 120 m. from a head-tank in nine lead pipes about 27 cm. in diameter which run across the lower part of the valley on a built substructure 17·4 m. high, and back up the other side. The head in at least two other of these siphons exceeds 75 m., whereas the highest surviving arched aqueduct, the Pont du Gard, is no more than 49 m. high.

But lead was not the only material used for pressure pipelines at this period; thick-walled clay pressure pipelines were also used in some circumstances, and are recommended by Vitruvius.[28] But one of the characteristic features of the water-supply

PLATE VIII

Oenoanda (Lycia): stone siphon pipes at the north end of the aqueduct

systems of Asia Minor is the use of stone pressure pipelines, with the Oenoanda system displaying a typical example. The water was taken across the saddle south of the city in a pipeline consisting of rough cubes of stone about 0·53 m. in each direction with a 0·17 m. hole cut through the middle (pl. VIII). The two end faces of each pipe block are dressed smooth and there is a socket at one end and a projecting lip at the other, so that with a mortar caulking they interlock to form a solid watertight tube. Stone, which is generally regarded as having a negligible tensile strength, is not a material that we would nowadays expect in this context, but in fact its use was seriously investigated by Thomas Telford in the nineteenth century for the water supply of Glasgow. He found that a 15 cm. pipe of Portland stone resisted a head of more than 100 m. of water, but the great drawback was unpredictability. Of two blocks tested from a quarry near Glasgow, one split at little more than 20 m. head, while another showed no sign of leakage with a 30 m. head.[29] In spite of this unpredictability, however, stone pressure pipelines were quite widely used under the Roman empire. Five instances have been reported in Italy, and three in North Africa, but, as the distribution map shows, they occur predominantly in the eastern half of the empire, with the heaviest concentration in western and south-western Asia Minor (fig. 22).[30] One reason for their popularity here is, of course, the ready availability of good-quality stone and the expertise to work it. This was an area where lead was less freely available than in the west for, although there are significant lead sources in Asia Minor (as shown on the distribution map), the main sources in the Roman period were in Britain, Gaul, Spain, Sardinia and Sicily.[31] At Oenoanda, for instance, a lead siphon would have required the purchase and import of some 50 tons of lead, which would need to be hauled up the steep and arduous road rising over 1,400 m. from the coast. The stone pipeline needed about 280 tons of stone, which was available within a kilometre of the required location with virtually no haulage uphill, and at no cost beyond the necessary labour. One can contrast the lavish use of 10,000 to 15,000 tons of lead for the siphons in the supply line to Roman Lyon.

In many cases no more than a note of the existence of these stone pipe blocks has been published. From those for which more detail is available it is apparent that their internal diameter might vary from 8·5 to 38 cm. according to the water supply concerned, and that the blocks were made about three times as high and wide as the intended bore, so that their wall thickness is about equal to their bore.[32] The length of the pipe blocks was often about equal to their width and height, as at Oenoanda, but this is less consistently the case. The lip and socket jointing of the blocks is simply an adaptation of the system long used in clay pipes, but a more curious technical feature is the slightly conical hole about 0·15 m. in diameter which occurs at intervals in a number of pipelines in the top face of the blocks.[33] At Laodicea and Aspendus the interval is apparently about 2·5 to 3 m., but in a not altogether reliable note on the Patara aqueduct by C. R. Cockerell, it is said to be 20 ft. (=6 m.). These holes would have to be closed when the pipeline was in operation, but their purpose is a mystery. Being set in the top of the pipeline, they would not be effective sludge cocks, while such narrow holes in such thick-walled pipes could not easily be used for rodding. The intervals are too short for branch pipes to be a reasonable explanation, but (except in one case) too great for the holes to be used in sealing the joints between blocks.

In even fewer cases is the hydraulic context of stone pipe blocks known—that is, the length and head of the inverted siphon to which they belong, and the constructions that went with it. Sometimes, the pipe-blocks were simply laid on a firm foundation at

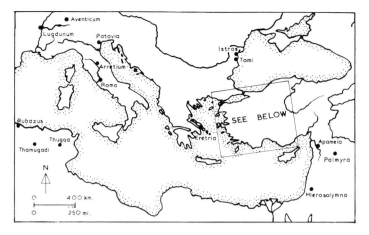

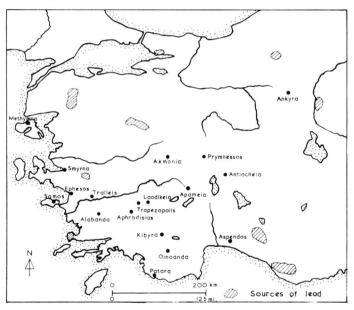

FIG. 22. Distribution map of stone siphon pipes

ground level, as at Jerusalem or Laodicea. But in what is perhaps the best-known example of the stone pressure pipeline, the one which supplied Aspendus in Pamphylia,[34] the pipe blocks are carried on a substantial arched aqueduct which is effectively horizontal between two pressure-release towers set at points where the line changes direction. The total length of the main pressure section is *c.* 924 m. with a head of 30 m., and the downward and upwards sections at either end are set at a slope of *c.* 30 degrees to avoid too abrupt a change of direction. The built aqueduct beneath the pressure pipeline obviously serves to smooth out the natural irregularities of the ground in the manner advised by Vitruvius, but it also reduces substantially the maximum head of water which the pipeline would have had to withstand if it had followed the ground level more closely. And the other alternative, a channel flowing at normal atmospheric pressure, would have added 30 m. to the height of the aqueduct over a length of 924 m., requiring the quarrying, transport and working of another 65,000 tons of stone.[35]

The same compromising approach can be seen on a smaller scale in the Oenoanda pipeline. The water had to be delivered in the city on a level of about 1,430 m., but it had first to cross a saddle at 1,401 m. It would have been possible in principle to build either an arched aqueduct 30 m. high and 500 m. long (or perhaps 700 m.; the position of the distribution tank is uncertain) or an inverted siphon at ground level, of the same length and subject to up to 30 m. head of pressure. In fact an aqueduct was built, but it was only 10 m., not 30 m., high, so its length needed to be no more than about 270 m. A pressure pipeline of the full length was also needed, but the maximum head was no more than 20 m. Thus, the expense of a long high aqueduct and the technical difficulties of higher pressure in the pipeline were both avoided.

The well-documented cases suggest that the maximum head considered viable with a stone pressure pipeline was substantially less than with lead pipes. Thus, at Oenoanda the head was 15 m. (later increased to 23 m.), at Patara it was *c.* 20 m., at Laodicea 25 m., at Aspendus 30 m., and at Jerusalem apparently *c.* 40 m. Much severer pressures have been suggested for the stone pipelines supplying Tralles (75 m.) and Smyrna (158 m.),[36] but these figures are based on the uncertain assumption that the water was delivered to the highest point in the city. Telford's experimental results, taken with the evidence of the better-attested instances mentioned above, justify serious scepticism until more evidence is forthcoming.

There has also been considerable argument about the date when the stone pressure pipelines were introduced in Asia Minor, and water supply systems are notoriously hard to date. The Aspendus system probably belongs in the second half of the second century A.D., and the high-level water supply to Jerusalem, with its pressure pipe section, was apparently also built in the second century A.D.[37] On the other hand, the certainly Hellenistic pressure pipes of Pergamum were of lead, of terracotta, or of terracotta with stone connecting-blocks, but not of stone by itself. One important, but inadequately studied, example of a stone pressure pipeline will probably shed some light on the matter in due course. It supplies the city of Patara in Lycia, and as at Oenoanda and Aspendus the stone pipeline runs across a built aqueduct which reduces the maximum pressure in the pipe blocks. It has often been thought pre-Roman, initially because of its massive polygonal masonry, but more recently because an inscription over one of the two small openings at its base records a repair by the emperor Vespasian.[38] However, both Waelkens and Farrington have pointed out that in Lycia this polygonal style of masonry continues into the second century A.D., and the inscribed block appears to be an integral part of the structure of the aqueduct, suggesting that the whole aqueduct was part of the Vespasianic reconstruction. The technology, form, and date of the supply system it replaced must remain uncertain, but the use of stone pressure pipes here need not be pre-Roman. Apart from these few instances where there is some direct evidence, the argument for the date of such stone pipelines turns on general considerations. On the one side are those who believe that the cities concerned, established or already flourishing in the Hellenistic period, must have required a sophisticated water supply early on; on the other are those who argue that since most cities did not reach their acme until the second century A.D., it is only under the Roman empire that they would need such systems.[39] The dispute is clearly inconclusive without further evidence.

Apart from this readiness to use a stone siphon tube even when an open channel on a built aqueduct would have been possible, the construction of aqueducts in Asia Minor involved no special techniques. The arch spans were normally 4·5–7 m. unless there was a river to be bridged, and the construction was normally in dressed stone, sometimes load-bearing, sometimes as a substantial facing to a rubble and mortar core. A mortared rubble facing was sometimes used, but brick is rare. There is much to be learnt about the circumstances which governed the choice of arched aqueduct, support wall, detour or siphon in crossing low ground, but until more supply systems have been surveyed as thoroughly as that of Pergamum, no such study can be undertaken.[40] We turn, therefore, from the technical to the economic and social factors which encouraged aqueduct construction.

It is clear that the cities of Asia Minor attached great importance to an impressive display of public building, and could call upon their wealthier citizens to express their wealth and patriotism by contributing generously to public building, and in some cases a single man might undertake the whole cost of a building. Given their value to the public, one might, therefore, have expected aqueducts, too, to be financed by wealthy individuals but this seems generally not to have been the case. Imperial involvement was often important, and familiarity with Rome's water supply may have encouraged emperors and their governors to back such projects. Thus, at Sardis Claudius built the water supply; at Balbura and Patara Vespasian or his governors sponsored construction or improvements, and Pliny's letters to Trajan attest his interest as Roman governor in the water supplies of Nicomedia and Sinope.[41] But local people seem less forthcoming. Surviving inscriptions may record gratitude to individuals for overseeing the construction of a water supply, no doubt a time-consuming and weighty responsibility; but it is almost always paid for by community funds.[42] The high cost may have been one reason for this,[43] but there is an obvious psychological motive, too. An architectural benefaction was intended as a permanent and public display of generosity, whereas the greater part of most water-supply lines lay at or below ground level, and so made no visual impact. Even the impressively raised sections were more likely to be in some remote valley far from roads and city, not crossing a major highway, like the aqueduct of Sextilius Pollio near Ephesus. A more attractive opportunity for displaying generosity was provided at the delivery point, where an elaborate fountain or nymphaeum might be built, as at Miletus. Thus at Hadriani in Mysia, a certain Aelius Philopappus supervised the construction of the water conduit from public funds, and limited his private contribution to the reconstruction of the fountain building.[44]

Finally, why were these innumerable new water-supply systems needed? It may seem self-evident that a better water supply is simply the route to a higher standard of living. In addition, it seems to be generally true that life in Asia Minor was becoming increasingly urbanized, with cities not just more prosperous, but more populous. But in some parts, at least, the process was far from complete. To return briefly to Oenoanda, evidence so far suggests that few people actually lived there during its monumental heyday.[45] And it must also be remembered that individual water requirements for drinking, cooking and washing amount to only a few litres a day.[46] No doubt the new aqueduct supplies did make living easier and more pleasant, and it is clear that both the Greeks and the Romans considered running spring water to be healthier than that from wells and cisterns. But there was, I believe, another more potent stimulus. Vitruvius emphasizes that water was essential not only for life itself and for daily uses, but also for pleasures, *delectationes*.[47] The sight of an elaborate nymphaeum was presumably one of these pleasures, but surely the most important was monumental bathing, and Mr Farrington's paper (pp. 50–9) shows how fully the inhabitants of Asia Minor adopted this Roman habit. Even small cities could not retain their self respect without at least one bath-building, for it was in such visible terms that rival cities measured their status. And although the early baths at Pompeii show that such bathing was possible without a major source of running water, the connections between bath building and the construction or repair of aqueducts, in both Rome and the provinces, are too numerous to be ignored.[48] I suggest, therefore, that the countless aqueducts of Roman Asia Minor are not due to Roman know-how nor, for the most part, to imitation of Rome. They were made possible by the Roman peace and its associated urban expansion, but the motivating force for their construction was to a large extent the spread of the Roman bathing habit.

NOTES

[1] Frontinus, *Aqu.* i.16.

[2] H. A. Thompson and R. E. Wycherley, *The Athenian Agora*, xiv: *The Agora of Athens* (Princeton, 1972), 197–200.

[3] H. Kienast, 'Der Tunnel des Eupalinos auf Samos', *Architectura*, vii (1977), 97–116.

[4] F. Graeber in *AvPerg*, i.3 (1913), 368–83; G. Garbrecht and H. Fahlbusch, *WAAPerg: die Madradag-Leitung*, LIWMitt, xxxvii (1973).

[5] Procopius, *BG*, i.19.13, 18; ii.9.1–11.

[6] Frontinus, *Aqu.* i.7; T. Ashby, *The Aqueducts of Rome* (Oxford, 1935), 88–158. The defensive advantage of a concealed conduit is noticed by Frontinus, *Aqu.* i.18.

[7] Frontinus, *Aqu.* i.7.

[8] Brief description and bibliography in C. Germain de Montauzan, *Les Aqueducs antiques de Lyon* (Paris, 1909), 194–6 and J. B. Ward-Perkins, 'The aqueduct of Aspendos', *PBSR*, xxiii (1955), 117, n. 4.

[9] H. Eschebach, *Pompeii: erlebte antike Welt* (Leipzig, 1978), 40; *id.*, 'Die innerstädtische Gebrauchswasserversorgung dargestellt am Beispiel Pompejis', *Aqueducs romains*, 85–7; R. Meiggs, *Roman Ostia*, 2nd edn. (Oxford, 1973), 44.

[10] The Aqua Julia (33 B.C.) and the Aqua Virgo (19 B.C.). The Aqua Julia and the earlier, but small, Aqua Tepula (125 B.C.) were both laid directly above the Aqua Marcia for most of their length.

[11] J.-M. Roddaz, *Marcus Agrippa* (Rome, 1984), 400. Some doubt is expressed by B. Gockel in Frontinus-Gesellschaft, *Wasserversorgung im antiken Rom* (Munich, 1982), 170.

[12] W. Wilberg, *FiE*, iii (1923), 156–65; the inscriptions are most recently treated in R. Merkelbach *et al.*, *IK*, xvii.1: *Die Inschriften von Ephesos*, vii.1 (1981), no. 3092.

[13] M. F. Smith, 'Diogenes of Oenoanda, New Fragments 122–124', *AS*, xxxiv (1984), 43–57, for the most recent fragments, with references to earlier publications.

[14] A. S. Hall, 'The Oenoanda Survey: 1974–76', *AS*, xxvi (1976), 191–7; *id.* in 'The year's work', *AS*, xxviii (1978), 5–6; *id.* in 'The year's work', *AS*, xxxii (1982), 5; *id.* in 'The year's work', *AS*, xxxiv (1984), 11–13; J. J. Coulton, 'The buildings of Oinoanda', *PCPS*, n.s. xxix (1983), 1–20.

[15] T. A. B. Spratt and E. Forbes, *Travels in Lycia, Milyas and the Cibyratis* (London, 1847), i, plan opp. p. 273.

[16] For a more detailed study of the Oenoanda water system see E. C. Stenton and J. J. Coulton, *AS*, xxxvi (1986), 15–59.

[17] A. M. Mansel, *Die Ruinen von Side* (Berlin, 1963), 49–52; U. Izmirligil, 'Die Wasserversorgungsanlagen von Side', *Historische Wasserversorgungsanlagen*, LIWMitt, lxiv (1979).

[18] A recent plan of Pergamum in *AvPerg*, xii: K. Nohlen and W. Radt, *Kapıkaya* (1978). The Roman

monumental buildings at the foot of the acropolis at Balbura are shown by Spratt and Forbes (*op. cit.* (note 15), plan opp. p. 267), but the Hellenistic walls round the hill above are not. For the plan of Limyra see C. Bayburtluoğlu, *Lycia* (Ankara, 1981), 25.

[19] The Augustan colony of Pisidian Antioch, established in an alien environment, was still given fortification walls (S. Mitchell in 'The year's work', *AS*, xxxiv (1984), 8–9).

[20] See note 17.

[21] G. Garbrecht and H. Fahlbusch, *WAAPerg: die Kaikos-Leitung*, LIWMitt, xliv (1975); K. Hecht, *WAAPerg: Zwei Aquädukte der Kaikos-Leitung*, LIWMitt, xlv (1975); *id.*, *WAAPerg: Zwei weitere Aquädukte der Kaikos-Leitung*, LIWMitt, liv (1976); *id.*, *Nochmals zwei Aquädukte der Kaikos-Leitung*, LIWMitt, lxi (1978).

[22] F. Rakob, 'Das Quellenheiligtum in Zaghouan und die römische Wasserleitung nach Karthago', *RömMitt*, lxxxi (1974), 41–51; *id.*, 'Die römische Wasserleitungen von Karthago', *Aqueducs romains*, 309–32.

[23] W. Haberey, *Die römischen Wasserleitungen nach Köln* (Düsseldorf, 1971).

[24] J. Schäfer *et al.*, *Phaselis* (Tübingen, 1981), 42–8.

[25] See, for example, A. T. Hodge, 'Siphons in Roman aqueducts', *PBSR*, li (1983), 180, n. 17.

[26] *Ibid.*, 194.

[27] On Roman siphons, Hodge, *op. cit.* (note 25), 174–221; H. Fahlbusch, *Vergleich antiker griechischer und römischer Wasserversorgungsanlagen*, LIWMitt, lxxiii (1982), 63–93. For those of Lyon, C. Germain de Montauzan, *op. cit.* (note 8), 59–71, 79–80, 90–3, 102–5, 118–22, 125–33, 176–220.

[28] Vitruvius, vii.6.10–11; examples in Spain are cited by Hodge, *op. cit.* (note 25), 190–1.

[29] Reported by D. Mackain, *Institution of Civil Engineers: Minutes of Proceedings*, ii (1843), 136.

[30] Full references are given in Stenton and Coulton, *op. cit.* (note 16).

[31] So J. F. Healy, *Mining and Metallurgy in the Greek and Roman World* (London, 1978), 61–2; for lead sources in Anatolia see P. S. de Jesus, *The Development of Prehistoric Mining and Metallurgy in Anatolia*, BAR S74 (Oxford, 1980), 64–9, maps 12–13.

[32] The largest bore is at Jerusalem (C. Schuck, 'Die Wasserversorgung der Stadt Jerusalem', *ZDPV*, i (1878), 160–4; A. Mazar, *Qadmoniot*, v (1972), 120–5 (Hebrew, with detailed contour map); *id.*, interviewed in *Biblical Archaeology Review*, x.3 (1984), 46–8).

[33] In continuous stretches of pipeline at Laodicea (spacing *c.* 1·5 m.), Patara (spacing *c.* 6 m.), Thugga (spacing *c.* 0·94 m.). Individual pipe-blocks with similar holes at Aspendus, Pisidian Antioch, and Smyrna.

[34] K. Lanckoronski *et al.*, *Städte Pamphyliens und Pisidiens*, i: *Pamphylien* (Vienna, 1890), 120–4; Ward-Perkins, *op. cit.* (note 8), 115–23.

[35] The maximum height, about 45 m., would have been less than that of the Pont du Gard, but there the length is only 275 m.

[36] So G. Weber, 'Die Wasserleitungen von Smyrna', *JDAI*, xiv (1899), 25; *id.*, 'Wasserleitungen in kleinasiatischen Städten', *JDAI*, xix (1904), 89–90.

[37] Aspendus: G. E. Bean, *Turkey's Southern Shore*, 2nd edn. (London, 1979), 53, based on *IGR*, iii, 804; Jerusalem: A. Mazar, interviewed in *Biblical Archaeology Review*, x.3 (1984), 48, on epigraphic grounds. R. Malinowski, 'Betontechnische Problemlosungen bei antiken Wasserbauten', *Historische Wasserversorgungsanlagen*, LIWMitt, lxiv (1979), table 2.2, attributes it to the time of Herod, while J. Wilkinson, 'Ancient Jerusalem: its water supply and population', *PEQ*, cvi (1974), 45–6, argues for a pre-Flavian date.

[38] Best account of this aqueduct by C. Texier, *Description de l'Asie Mineure*, iii (Paris, 1849), 192–3, 224, pl. 179; some further information and a highly distorted sketch derived from C. R. Cockerell in *Institution of Civil Engineers: Minutes of Proceedings*, xiv (1855), 206–8; see also Fahlbusch, *op. cit.* (note 27), 84, fig. 50. The inscription is mentioned by R. Malinowski and H. Fahlbusch, 'Untersuchungen des Dichtungsmortels von fünf geschichtlichen Rohrleitungen im ägäisch-anatolischen Raum', *Wasser im antiken Hellas*, LIWMitt, lxxi (1981), 208.

[39] G. Weber, 'Wasserleitungen in kleinasiatischen Städten', *JDAI*, xx (1905), 209, summarizing a series of earlier articles, argues for a Hellenistic date; Fahlbusch (*op. cit.* (note 27), 56, 66, 84) inclines to accept a Hellenistic date for the Patara stone pipeline, and perhaps that of Smyrna, but a Roman date for the remainder. A. von Gerkan, *Griechische Städteanlagen* (Berlin, 1924), 89–90, and A. W. van Buren, *RE*, vii.A (1955), 472–5, prefer a Roman date. Note that Alexandria Troas still relied on wells and cisterns at the time of Hadrian (Philostratus, *Vitae Soph.* (ed. Kayser), 56.22–4).

[40] The possibilities are well shown by K. Hecht 'Baugeschichtliche Betrachtungen zu einigen

Aquädukten der Kaikosleitung von Pergamon', *Historische Wasserversorgungsanlagen*, LIWMitt, lxiv (1979).

[41] Sardis: *IGR*, iv, 1505; Balbura: C. Naour, 'Nouvelles inscriptions de Balboura', *Ancient Society*, ix (1978), 166–70; Patara: see note 38 above; Pliny, *Ep.* 10.37–8, 90–1. Note also Smyrna: *IGR*, iv, 1411–12 (Trajan's father); Ephesus: C. Börker and R. Merkelbach, *IK*, xii: *Die Inschriften von Ephesos*, ii (1979), nos. 401, 402; Nicaea: S. Şahin, *IK*, ix: *Katalog der antiken Inschriften des Museums von Iznik*, i (1979), nos. 1, 55; Alexandria Troas: Philostratus, *Vitae Soph.* (ed. Kayser), 56.21–30 (Hadrian); Amaseia: F. and E. Cumont, *Studia Pontica*, iii (1910), no. 100 (repair). Imperial encouragement, Ephesus: Börker and Merkelbach, *op. cit.* (this note), nos. 415, 416.

[42] Community funds: Börker and Merkelbach, *op. cit.* (note 41), no. 402 (Ephesus); 'Funde', *AthMitt*, xxi (1896), 84–5, no. 9.8–9; Pliny, *Ep.* 10.37 (Claudiopolis); *IGR*, iii, 848 (Olbia, with help from a bequest ?); *IGR*, iv, 1491 (Kassaba); M. Gough, 'Anazarbus', *AS*, ii (1952), 149, nos. 1–2 (Anazarbus); L. Robert, *Hellenica*, ix (1950), 28–38 (village near Philadelphia); G. Petzl, 'Antike Zeugnisse aus der Umgebung von Thyateira', *ZPE*, xxiii (1976), 243–50, no. 1 (village near Thyateira). Private finance: Merkelbach *et al.*, *op. cit.* (note 12), no. 3092, Börker and Merkelbach, *op. cit.* (note 41), no. 424 (both Ephesus); W. Ameling, *IK*, xxvii: *Die Inschriften von Prusias ad Hypium* (1985), no. 20 (Prusias ad Hypium); G. Deschamps and G. Cousin, 'Inscriptions du temple de Zeus Panamaros', *BCH*, xii (1888), 84–5, no. 9.8–9 (Stratonicea); W. M. Calder, 'A journey round the Proseilemmene', *Klio*, x (1910), 235; *IGR*, iv, 1653 (village near Philadelphia; see also L. Robert, *Hellenica*, ix (1950), 30, n. 3). *IGR*, iii, 804 (Aspendus; here an impressive built aqueduct easily visible from the city); Philostratus, *Vitae Soph.* (ed. Kayser), 56.30–4 (Alexandria Troas; the family of Herodes Atticus making good their overspending on an imperial project).

[43] At Rome the Aqua Claudia and the Anio Novus together cost 55,500,000 sestertii or 13,875,000 den. (Pliny, *NH*, xxxvi.24). In Asia Minor the aqueduct at Alexandria Troas cost at least 7,000,000 dr. (Philostratus, *Vitae Soph.* (ed. Kayser), 50.31), that at Aspendus at least 2,000,000 den. (*IGR*, iii, 804), while 3,329,000 sestertii (=841,125 den.) were spent on an abortive scheme at Claudiopolis (Pliny, *Ep.* 10.37); but at Eumenea a water channel cost only 3,812 den. (*MAMA*, iv, 333).

[44] *IGR*, iv, 242. And at Ephesus Sextilius Pollio supervised (with a colleague) the construction of a new supply, but only paid for the very visible aqueduct (above, p. 73 and note 12); compare Börker and Merkelbach, *op. cit.* (note 41), 402.

[45] Coulton, *op. cit.* (note 14), 4, n. 13.

[46] About 25–50 litres per person per day is used in Third World water systems where water is to be collected from a standpipe, although the figure varies substantially in different continents (R. J. Saunders and J. J. Warford, *Village Water Supplies* (Baltimore, 1976), 124). With the perpetually flowing fountains of a Graeco-Roman system, a large part of the inflow (perhaps nearly half) would flow away unused except in flushing the drains.

[47] Vitruvius, viii.1.1.

[48] Rome: Ashby, *op. cit.* (note 6), 14; Ostia: Meiggs, *op. cit.* (note 9), 44, 406; Carthage: F. Rakob, 'Die römische Wasserleitungen von Karthago', *Aqueducs romains*, 309–10, 318; Aspendus: Ward-Perkins, *op. cit.* (note 8), 122–3; Patara: Coulton, *op. cit.* (note 14), 9. The connection is also made by Philostratus, *Vitae Soph.* (ed. Kayser), 56.20–4.

Social Correlations to the Greek Cavea in the Roman Period

D. B. Small

I would like to take a rather unconventional approach to the topic of Greek theatres in the Roman east. I have for a long time thought that a symbolic approach, tackling the issue of the correlation between the spatial composition of Greek caveae and the social structure of their communities would yield interesting and, it is hoped, fruitful results.

I therefore propose to begin my study with a spatial analysis of these caveae. Athough relatively new to classical archaeology, spatial analysis has produced stimulating results in other archaeological fields.[1] In this paper I would like to show how a spatial approach to Greek caveae in the Roman period provides meaningful correlations between the theatre and culture, and how this approach posits promising research designs for future work in Roman Greece.

The Greek cavea

There were few theatres built in the periods when the Greek east was part of the empire. Except for some advances such as circular *cryptoportici*, the cavea designs are a continuation of those built in theatres of the Classical and Hellenistic periods. If I had to choose a typical Roman-period cavea, I would select the Odeion of Herodes Atticus in Athens (fig. 23). On the south-west slope of the Acropolis, this odeion was built by Herodes in the later part of the second century A.D. to the memory of his wife, Regilla. Most of the marble facing and the *scaenae frons* were removed from the building before it was cleared in the nineteenth century. But the cavea is well enough preserved to allow us to define its spatial arrangement.

The cavea of this odeion was divided into two large sections by an intervening walkway. The lower section was divided into five principal and two truncated

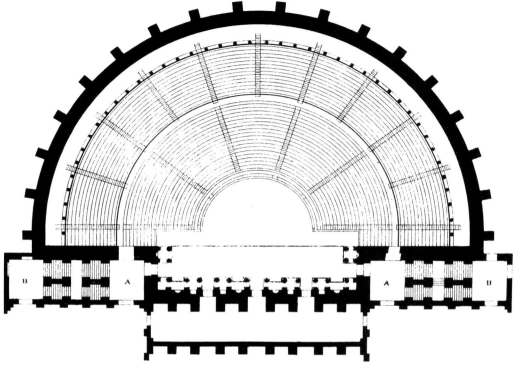

Fig. 23. The Odeion of Herodes Atticus in Athens (from P. Versakis, 'Mnemeia ton notion propodon tes Akropoleos', *Ephemeris archaiologike* (1912), pl. 8)

kerkides, or wedge-shaped sections, by radiating stairways. The additional stairways in the upper cavea divided it in turn into twelve *kerkides*, ten major and two minor on its ends. Although we have no remaining evidence of chairs, a possible single row of *proedria*, or privileged seats, ran along the edge of the lower walkway on the rim of the orchestra.

The social correlations

The spatial features of this type of cavea may be correlated to the social structure of the community. Textual, epigraphic, and numismatic evidence argue that these spatial arrangements were correlated to different segments of the community's society. Admittedly, this evidence is chronologically diffuse, i.e. coming variously from the Classical, Hellenistic, and Roman periods, but the design of Greek caveae changed very little from Classical to Roman times. The evidence appears to apply well to the majority of theatres, both early and late.

The division of the cavea into *kerkides* appears to be correlated to two levels of group distinction. The first and most basic was that between citizen and metic. Non-citizens might have been relegated to the *kerkides* furthest from centre. This division is suggested by a fragment (41K) from a comedy by Alexis of Thurii in which a woman grumbles that she had to take a seat in the outermost *kerkis*, like a foreigner. The second level of separation is tribal. We have several pieces of evidence that point to different tribes sitting in tribally distinct *kerkides*. Frequently-found small, round, coin-like tokens, which may be called tickets for lack of better definition, show that different *kerkides* of a Greek cavea were assigned to different tribes.[2] Although many of these 'tickets' are probably from earlier periods, it appears that the *kerkides* were still correlated to this tribal division after Rome's domination. The theatre at Megalopolis has names of different tribes marking the different *kerkides* of the cavea. Epigraphers suggest that they were inscribed in the late first century B.C.[3] Athens shows a similar trend. When Hadrian visited in A.D. 126, each tribe dedicated a statue in their section of the cavea of the Theatre of Dionysus to the emperor.[4]

The spatial distinction between *proedria* and the remaining sections of the cavea is correlated to hierarchical division. These seats were inscribed with the offices of the city or priests' positions. It is important to note here that, with very few exceptions, the inscriptions found on these chairs are only titles without specific names. They were for the current magistrates or priests and not specific individuals. It was the post, then, and not the individual that was separated from the rest of the assembly.

This spatial arrangement correlates with the groups in Greek communities up to a point. But then the correlation falls short. In Athens, where we have the best understanding of society during the later periods, we know that these spatial features do not reflect the full picture of Athenian social division in Roman times. This disjunction is seen in two ways. First, there were more groups with various hierarchical divisions in the community than those reflected in the citizen/metic or privileged post/rest seating distinction in the spatial arrangement of the cavea. If I understand the historians correctly, there were many hierarchically divided groups in Roman Athens and structural differentiation, i.e. the appearance of new groups or the change in status of older ones, was slow, but ongoing.[5] For example, the Areopagites had come to hold perhaps the most privileged social position. There might even have been a rebirth in power of noble families, the old *gennetai*, who were now travelling in the guise of *curiales*. The second point is that the structure of the hierarchical differentiation in the cavea does not adequately reflect the structure of the hierarchical grouping within the Athenian community. Although the social structure was evolving, the presence and position of elite groups like the Areopagites was 'stabilized' for successive generations. The *proedria*, although distinct from the rest of the cavea, were ostensibly open to several status groups within this hierarchical community structure, not just one, and therefore would not reflect the positions and relations of the different groups within the community.

This disruption of correlation between both the larger number of status groups and their type of differentiation in the social aggregate and that reflected in the architectural arrangement of the cavea is best explained by a socio-cultural model of Athenian society which defines the society as a loosely articulated social structure in which diverse social settings were permitted to develop their own norms and conventions. Humphreys[6] defines such a social setting well as 'a concrete interaction-context defined for actors by spatio-temporal segregation and/or symbolic scene-making devices, and associated with a particular set of roles and behavioural norms'. The dynamics of this loose articulation of social settings rest in strong differentiation between the settings themselves. Often there are rites, ceremonies, or symbolic settings that seek to mark the differentiation of roles and settings for the community. The social setting for the cavea was public assembly, the dominant setting for the city. Athenian society employed symbols to mark the transition from other roles and settings to the setting of the assembly and its specific roles. Role-defining oaths, such as those taken upon gaining office or that of the ephebes, which called upon Athenians to enter politics as equals, leaving behind other interests, served as transition markers between these and other roles in the community. Just as the others marked the role differentiation, the egalitarian architectural image, i.e. the spatial arrangement of the cavea with its paucity of hierarchical spatially distinguished seating and its status section, and the *proedria*, not fixed to the hierarchical structure of the community, marked the differentiation of the public assembly from other social settings.

The potential for future research in the Roman east

What significance does this have to us as archaeologists concerned with Greece under Roman domination? I would argue that the distribution of the Greek caveae in the Roman period supplies us with unique opportunities for developing research designs for the study of social structure in the communities in which they are found. Initially, I would suggest that we can look at this social model in many different contexts by studying archaeological correlations to different groups in these communities. We could study the presence, growth, and possible competition of such groups through the study of mortuary data, seriation of what we know were prestige goods, and demography. If we could build a body of data from many different contexts, we might be able some day to step beyond the correlations and propose models for stability and change in this social structure itself.

We stand in an extremely advantageous position for pursuing such research. We have an almost unparalleled archaeological and textual database. There is a wide geographical distribution of examples of this cavea, a long history of its continuity, and a good general text-based knowledge of societies in the Roman Empire. And, unlike many other archaeologists, most notably of the prehistoric period, who must often build models from the archaeological record, we can begin with a text-based model, which is quite well developed.

Our approach could be both synchronic and diachronic. Synchronically we could add to the understanding of this social model in many different environments. The fact that we find similar examples of caveae in such faraway places as Hellenistic cities in Asia Minor urges us to consider that the dynamics of the differentiation of roles and social settings in the social structure of these distributed communities were similar to those which we observed in Athens. The reasons for this might centre around whether these communities grew synchronically from the same broad cultural background as Athens or were later Hellenistic foundations.

Although this synchronic research is important, the diachronic approach, the study of the changes and differentiation in the various social settings or roles through time, is just as promising. At present I see this study having two foci, one concerning the ability of the system to retain its basic dynamics and the other the change in the dynamics themselves. For the first, frequent examples of the continuation of this type of cavea into the Roman period, seen in cities such as Sagalassus (fig. 24),[7] argue strongly that the dynamics of social setting and role differentiation in the communities in which we find them were not significantly changing over time. We could argue this at least until the third century A.D., when work on theatres all but ceased.

On the other hand, we do have a few examples that suggest a change in the

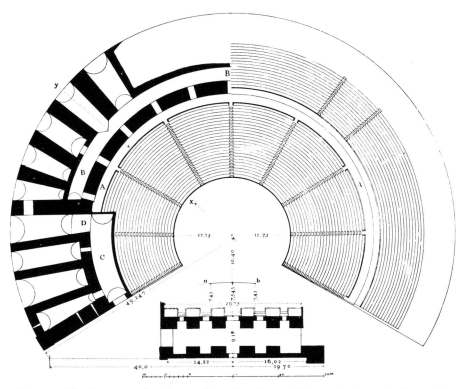

FIG. 24. The theatre at Sagalassus (from Lanckoronski, *op. cit.* (note 7), fig. 127)

dynamics of the community's social differentiation. At present I know of two examples where a study of the caveae argues that the dynamics had broken down. One of
these communities is Stobi.[8] Founded in the late third or early second century B.C., the
city's condition continued relatively unchanged until it began to expand rapidly
during the reign of Augustus. It appears to have undergone a second period of
development in the second and third centuries A.D. By A.D. 69 Stobi was a
municipium civium Romanorum. The cavea of the city's theatre is like those we have
discussed (fig. 25). But in a significant departure, excavation has uncovered hundreds
of inscriptions, carved on the seats (fig. 26). The full report of the excavation of the
theatre has yet to be published, but we may see some of the examples of inscriptions
that were found in the thirties, when the first three *kerkides* of the left side of the cavea
were uncovered. Like some of the inscriptions in the theatres already mentioned,
many of these inscriptions are tribal, denoting sections of the cavea for certain tribes.
But a large percentage are of personal and family names. Their presence is a
significant break from the other inscriptions found in caveae elsewhere, which might
denote a seat only for a certain privileged post. Static groups were now being spatially
distinguished in the cavea. The egalitarian image was broken. The assembly was now
not differentiated in respect to status structure from other social settings in the
community. Because the construction of the cavea may antedate the period of the first
inscriptions, Stobi offers us an excellent chance to examine change within the

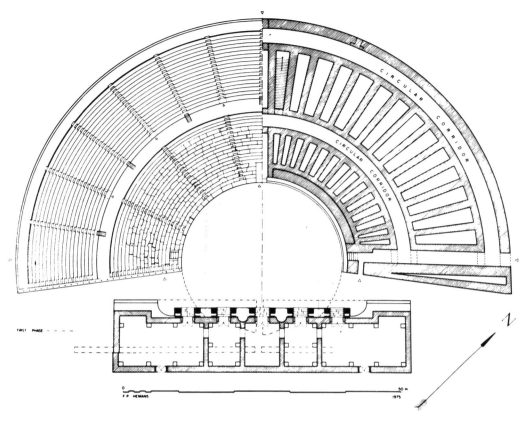

FIG. 25. The theatre at Stobi (from Wiseman, *op. cit.* (note 8), fig. 4)

community before and after the breakdown in the dynamics of the separation of the assembly setting from other settings in the community.

The second community is Termessus.[9] Originally a Pisidian community in southern Turkey, this city appears to have undergone traceable Greek acculturation after Alexander's conquests. In an inscription from the second century B.C. she even refers to herself as a democracy. Little is known of Termessus in the Roman Empire. But from a quick look at its necropolis and some of its monuments, it would be safe to say that it was prosperous at least until the third century A.D. Its theatre dates from the Hellenistic period. During the Empire its cavea was enlarged by an upper section and the scene building was attached to the auditorium. In the upper section of the cavea there are many inscriptions, some referring to priests or perhaps officials, but, significantly, several are names of specific persons (fig. 27). The situation thus appears to be similar to that at Stobi. The absence of inscriptions in the theatre before the Imperial cavea addition argues that there was an ongoing differentiation in social setting, and that it, too, had weakened in the Imperial period. Termessus still awaits archaeological research, but the fact that only the upper section of the cavea received the inscriptions is immediately fascinating. Was there an additional tacit separation of people between upper and lower sections?

KERKIS 1

ROW	FACE	LIP	TOP
2	—	—	1 ΛΟΥΚΙΟΥ / ΚΥΝΤΙ 2 Φ ΝΙΟΥ / ΠΟΒΛ ϹΕΡΙ / ΠΑΥΛ ठ / ΑΙΛΙ Ϲ[..]Λ 3 ΚΟΥΝΤΙΛΙ / ΚΟΡΝ ΠΑΥΛΙ ΑΓΑΘΟΚΛΕΟϹ / Λ 4 ΕΝΑΝΑϹ Ϲ
3			5 ΟΥΗΒΙ 6 αΛ / ΛΕ 7 ΕΠΙΘΥΜΗΤΟΥ Υ ΓΑΙΟ / ϹΑΒΕΙ ΝΟΥ 8 ΛठΚΙठ
4		9 ΦΥΛΙ ΜΑΡΤΙΑϹ 10 ΦΥΛΗϹ ΟΥΑΛΕΡΙΑϹ	11 ΦΥ 12 Ἄ ΓΑΙ / ΚΟΙ
5		17 ΦΥ Κ..ΙΑΙ 18 Β	13 ΦΙ 14 ⋄ΑΛ 15 ΔΙ 16 ठ
6			19 Monogram 20 ठ
7	22 ΥΚ⊳ΡΧ 18ΛΙ	21 Γ ΠΕΥ 21a ΧΙ / ΤΡΙ / [...]ΕΙΒ ΒΛϹ	23 ΕΥΧΑ ΠΡΕΠ 24 ΕΙΟΥ ΕΟΥΙ ω ΚΛΟΥ
8		26 ΠΟ ΑΙ	ΛΕ Ξ/Ο ΕΥΤΥ / ΤΝΡ Κ 25 ΕΙΘΑΓΕΝωΝ
9	Χ	ΤᴗΛ	27 ΚΡΑΤΟΑΥΜठ / ΓΑΙΟΥ ΟΥΑ[... ΔΩ 28 ΟΥΑΡΙωΝ 29 ΙΟΥΛΙΑΝωΝ ΚΑΙ 30 ΠΕΤΙΛΛΙΟΥ ΓΑΙΑΝΟΥ
10		31 [Σ]ΕΚΟΥΝΛΟ 31a α[..]Ο ΦΟΙΠϹ 31b Α ΛΥ Φ ΚΡ/... ΝᴑΥ Ε//\///	32 ΚΡΑΤωΝΟΥ 33 ΠΟΜϹωΤΗ[ρ]ΙΧठΓ 34 ΛΕΙΒΙΥ (=Λειβί(ο)υ) 35 Ι Ο ΝᴑΜϹ 36 ΝΕΙ(χίου?) ΝΕΙ ΝΕΙΚΙᴑΥ Β

Fig. 26. Some names on the seats in the theatre at Stobi (from Saria, *op. cit.* (note 8), fig. 3)

In looking for the causes of such a breakdown in setting and role differentiation as in Stobi and Termessus, I think it would be worthwhile to turn our attention to Italy. As a result of the intrusion of the punitive Roman colony in 81 B.C., Pompeii had undergone many significant social changes. Changes in the design of the cavea of the large theatre argue that one of these was a breakdown in the differentiation dynamics of the separation of the assembly from other social settings here as well (fig. 28).[10] The large theatre was built before Sulla's colony. What we know of its original character shows that it was like our Greek caveae and not significantly spatially status-divided. But in the Augustan period there was change. The duumviri M. Holconius Rufus and M. Holconius Celer built a *crypta* and *tribunalia* into the cavea. Besides providing a slope for caveae, *cryptae* were used by Roman architects to direct traffic to different status-correlated sections of the auditorium, i.e. the upper and lower parts of the cavea and seats in the orchestra, which were portioned out to senators, knights and magistrates; and the *tribunalia*, which were given to persons of highest distinction. The whole cavea was now status-divided and fixed to the status structure of the

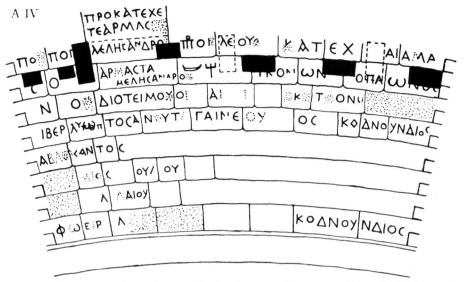

FIG. 27. Some names from the seats in the theatre at Termessus (from *TAM*, 872 A IV)

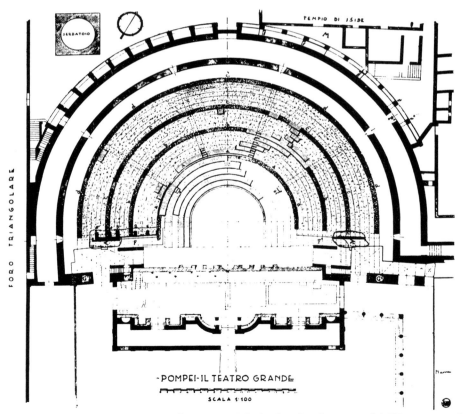

FIG. 28. The large theatre at Pompeii (from A. Maiuri, 'Saggi nella cavea del "Teatro grande"', *Notizie degli Scavi*, ser. 8, v (1951), fig. 2)

community. The old differentiation between the assembly and other social settings was broken down.

The importance of this change in Pompeii for archaeologists lies both in the great abundance of archaeological material and in our greater knowledge of its social correlations. A close look at Pompeii might aid us in understanding the dynamics of the changes at Stobi and Termessus.

Conclusion

In sum, this paper has stressed the importance of the correlation of the spatial arrangement of the cavea to the social structure of the community. A concentration on this correlation, I believe, would give us an opportunity to investigate the social dynamics of many of these communities and provide important contributions to future research in the Roman east.

NOTES

[1] See, for example, R. Fletcher, 'Settlement studies (micro and semi-micro)', in D. L. Clarke (ed.), *Spatial Archaeology* (London, 1977), 47–162; D. G. Saile, 'Architecture in prehispanic Pueblo archaeology; examples from Chaco Canyon', *World Archaeology* (1980), 156–74; D. Preziosi, *Minoan Architectural Design, Formation and Signification* (Berlin, 1983).

[2] A. W. Pickard-Cambridge, *The Dramatic Festivals of Athens* (Oxford, 1953), 272–5, figs. 205–6.

[3] H. Homolle, 'Le théâtre de Megalopolis', *JHS*, xi (1890), 55–71.

[4] *IG*, iii, 466–69.

[5] J. H. Oliver, 'From *Gennetai* to *Curiales*', *Hesperia*, xlix (1980), 30–56.

[6] S. Humphreys, *Anthropology and the Greeks* (London, 1978), 249.

[7] K. Lanckoronski, *Städte Pamphyliens und Pisidiens*, ii: *Pisidien* (Vienna, 1892), 152–4, figs. 127–37.

[8] E. R. Gebhard, 'The Theatre at Stobi: a summary', in B. Aleksova and J. Wiseman (eds.), *Studies in the Antiquities of Stobi*, iii (Skopje, 1981), 13–27; J. Wiseman, 'A distinguished Macedonian family of the Roman Imperial period', *AJA*, lxxxviii (1984), 567–82, fig. 4.; for the inscriptions: B. Saria, 'Die Inschriften des Theaters von Stobi', *Wiener Jahreshefte*, xxxii (Beibl.) (1940), 3–34.

[9] G. E. Bean, *Turkey's Southern Shore* (London, 1969), 119–37; D. De Bernardi-Ferrero, *Teatri Classici in Asia Minore*, ii (Rome, 1971), 2–31, with accompanying plan.

[10] There are many accounts of the theatre, but they are best summarized by M. Bieber, *The History of Greek and Roman Theater* (Princeton, 1961), 170–3, figs. 607–8.

The Adoption of Roman Building Techniques in the Architecture of Asia Minor

Marc Waelkens*

Despite the fact that the actual number of well-preserved architectural remains is probably larger in Asia Minor than in almost any other part of the Roman Empire, even including Italy, there is still no concise summary covering all aspects of its building techniques.[1] This is mainly due to a lack of proper recording of what still can be seen on hundreds of unexcavated sites. It is also due to the fact that most of the older excavation reports were concerned with the general layout and decoration of buildings, rather than with a detailed description of the technical aspects of their construction. Yet, certain broad tendencies have already emerged from the available evidence and one may cautiously venture to summarize them here.

By Roman building techniques we mean essentially the use of cemented walls and the replacement of ashlar masonry by a concrete-like structure with or without a facing.[2] In Greek architecture, including that of Asia Minor, lime mortar was already known from the Classical period onwards, in a wide variety of circumstances, especially as a hydraulic sealing, in the joints of fortification walls, or as a bedding for the bottom course of foundations.[3] Sometimes the Hellenistic East also seems to have used a kind of 'pseudo-concrete' made of broken stones held together with lime mortar.[4] On the whole, however, before the middle of the first century B.C., lime mortar or pseudo-concrete in Asia Minor was not really put to any structural use, at least not in monumental architecture. The use of lime-mortared rubble walls required a radical revision of the standard Hellenistic building practices, whose strength had been based solely on ashlar construction, which determined, by its mass and attendant structural problems, the whole concept of a building and emphasized the architecture of the exterior. With the more flexible Roman building techniques, which eliminated most of the earlier structural problems, there was a growing awareness of the properties of interior space, which from now on determined the planning of a building.[5] Concrete-like walls or structures became widespread in the architecture of

Asia Minor from the time of the revival of the building industry under Augustus, and may have derived from Italy, or at least been the result of direct Roman influence, although they rarely acquired the strength of Roman concrete and are better described as 'mortared rubble'.[6]

Yet these architectural innovations did not reach the whole of the peninsula at the same time, nor did they everywhere affect building activities to the same extent. However, there is only space to mention the most important or characteristic monuments here.

The progressive introduction of what we have called 'Roman' building techniques is best documented in the area of the western coastlands. In Pergamum there was already a tradition of using lime-mortar for specific purposes before it was incorporated into the Roman Empire in 133 B.C.[7] Here, apparently during the reign of Augustus, the Pergamenes rebuilt a Hellenistic gymnasium in the central part of the city. Whereas the original building possessed dry walls of irregular stones, the newly erected walls were made of mortared rubble between two facings of small rectangular stones set in a mortar bed, resembling the 'petit appareil' of Gaul.[8] To my knowledge they are thus far the earliest evidence for the application of this particular technique in Asia Minor. Yet, generally speaking, it seems to have been applied only reluctantly in Pergamene architecture of the early Imperial period.[9] The triumph of the new building techniques finally occurred under Hadrian. In the Hadrianic renovation of the Upper Gymnasium most corners, arches and vaults were still built of ashlar or well-cut blocks set in mortar with smaller stones masking a concrete core,[10] but in the renovation of the Asklepieion, perhaps begun at the instigation of the emperor himself when he visited the sanctuary in A.D. 123, concrete was applied in a more progressive way. The Temple of Asclepius Soter is directly modelled on the Pantheon, and its building methods and materials are a blend of local and imported Roman techniques. Its foundations thus consist of an ashlar facing, partly penetrating one of the hardest concrete cores known from Asia Minor. The drum, however, instead of using the carefully graded, brick-faced concrete of the Roman prototype, was built of fine ashlar in the traditional way. Yet, full mastery of the new techniques reappeared in the dome, built of radially set fired bricks, possibly alternating with concrete sections and certainly reinforced at the springing by an outer ring of mortared rubble.[11] The slightly later adjoining semi-subterranean rotunda has walls made of a mortared rubble core, faced with small cut stones. The piers, supporting two annular concrete vaults with a radially laid fieldstone facing, are built either of solid ashlar or of ashlar quoins and 'petit appareil' sections. The upper drum of the building consisted of ashlar piers with a cemented rubble infill and a series of apsides in mortared rubble, faced with small blocks. They supported ashlar arches and most probably concrete half-domes.[12] During the reign of Hadrian, Pergamum also received one of the most important brick buildings of the peninsula, namely the Temple of the Egyptian Gods. Whereas its round flanking towers are built of mortared rubble faced with the (by then) common squared blocks of andesite, the great central hall is constructed of brick throughout.[13] At Pergamum, walls of mortared rubble alternating with brick bonding courses running through the entire thickness, a common device in early Byzantine architecture, can already be found in a latrine of the Antonine period.[14]

At Ephesus, which became the undisputed metropolis of Asia, Roman building techniques seem to have been introduced towards the middle of the first century B.C.

A still experimental phase can be seen in the circular Tropaion on the Panayir Daği, perhaps built to commemorate Pompey's victories over the pirates. Its lower section has a core of small, roughly cut stones set in lime mortar.[15] Two monuments, probably built under Marcus Antonius, already announce standard building practices of the Augustan period. The temple on the State Agora, possibly built by the triumvir himself, had its walls and columns supported by ashlar foundations embedded in a concrete-like rubble mass,[16] a technique which is repeated in the early Augustan Temple of Caesar and Roma, erected by the Italic residents of the city.[17] The Octagon, also dated to the time of Marcus Antonius, has pseudo-isodomic ashlar slabs around a core of mortared rubble.[18] The same structural system can be found in several Augustan monuments at Ephesus, such as the monument for C. Memmius, grandson of Sulla,[19] and the bridge of the aqueduct built by C. Sextilius Pollio, a curator sent by the emperor himself. The sections of its arches in dressed stone, carried by piers with an ashlar facing around a mortared rubble fill, are built in the same manner, while its abutments and superstructure consist of mortared rubble faced with smaller irregular stones.[20] Other applications of the technique occur in the lower part of the basilica, again built by Pollio and his family, and in the monument dedicated to him by his step-son.[21]

In all these buildings the influence of the Hellenistic 'emplekton' walls, with their earth and rubble fill between ashlar facings, is still apparent in the fact that the facing slabs or blocks do penetrate into the concrete core. Therefore they have not yet become a mere facing, but still have a stabilizing function. Even the retaining walls of the theatre, repaired in the second half of the first century, still betray the influence of Hellenistic architecture. In fact, they consist of an outer facing of smoothly dressed ashlar, joined by metal clamps, and an inner layer of roughly cut stones without clamps, set against a core of mortared rubble. Part of the Stadium, dated to the reign of Nero, is supported on a barrel-vaulted substructure built of large unworked fieldstones set in a mortared rubble fill.[22] We have to wait until the Flavian period to find concrete-like walls faced with squared blocks of the 'petit appareil' type being used in monumental architecture, in the two-storeyed vaulted substructure of the Temple of Domitian.[23] In the late Trajanic library built in honour of Ti. Julius Celsus Polemaeanus by his son (both men former consuls), the main walls were of coarse local marble up to a height of 4 m. The rest of the walls were of solid brick throughout. The library thus becomes the earliest known building in the peninsula to use solid brick walls.[24] These were most probably used because the commissioner, who had spent part of his career at Rome, wanted to imitate the *opus latericium* of the capital in order to express his own Romanitas. Solid brick walls eventually became very widespread at Ephesus. Besides an early second-century remodelling of the Domitianic Harbour Baths, the superstructures, including arches and vaults, of several other bath buildings of the earlier second century, are built by the same technique.[25] In later baths, such as those built by P. Vedius Antoninus towards the middle of the century, ashlar is used in heavy piers and at corners, while the rest of the complex is built of mortared rubble faced with smaller stones.[26]

Thus, even in the second century, ashlar continued to be used for all supportive elements, while lime-mortared walls, mortared rubble and brick walls were confined to less important, non-structural sections. 'Petit appareil' sections alternating with brick bonding courses appear at Ephesus towards the end of the second century.[27]

At Sardis the adoption of Roman building techniques may have progressed at a faster pace. This may be partly due to a pre-existing local tradition of walls in mortared rubble.[28] But it was above all the rebuilding of the city after the massive earthquake of A.D. 17 which made possible several experiments in the new building techniques, displaying a greater variety than most of the contemporary structures at Pergamum and Ephesus. It is also significant that the rebuilding of the city was carried out by a special commissioner sent from Rome, who probably had architects to hand, some of whom may have been trained in the capital.[29] Thus, in the theatre there was an attempt to devise a flexible wall system to counteract earthquake shocks. In fact the core of the western parodos wall displays a strange combination of alternating irregular ashlar-faced piers running through the entire thickness of the wall and concrete-like sections of mortared rubble.[30] Other first-century buildings are made of cemented field- or riverstones.[31] Even 'petit appareil' facing is used here. It already occurs in the possibly first-century A.D. foundations of the large terrace supporting the enormous Bath-Gymnasium complex. The older, western, section of the complex, whose construction may have started in the second half of the first century or in the first half of the second, also has walls built using this technique.[32] However, the Antonine and Severan central part used a structural system in which all the loads were transferred on to smaller piers of solid ashlar, fitted together with metal clamps, using no (or minimal) mortar, and larger piers of mortared rubble faced with blocks of cut stone. The wall sections above and between the piers consisted of a careless fill of rubble, often using very little mortar, held in place by a facing of fieldstone laid in orderly horizontal rows, alternating with bands of bricks going through the entire wall. The arches were of brick, the keystones of ashlar, and the vaults of radially laid brick.[33] Similar ashlar and cemented fieldstone combinations, sometimes used in conjunction with brick bonding-courses, and supporting either solid stone or brick vaults and arches, occur in two other second- or early third-century bath buildings.[34] Thus, the architects active in second-century Sardis eventually developed a construction system which was similar to that of their contemporaries at Pergamum and Ephesus.

Another of the bigger cities of Asia, Miletus, betrays all the conservatism of a city which had passed its prime, not only in its planning, but also in its building techniques. Lime mortar makes it first appearance here in the Big Harbour Monument, built either for Pompey or for Augustus. Its foundations are basically a filling of earth and rubble, in which mortar is only used as a levelling device, not as an adhesive.[35] The same sparing use of lime mortar is characteristic of all early Imperial buildings.[36] One has to wait until the reign of Claudius before Roman building techniques really make their appearance in the baths built by Cn. Vergilius Capito, a Roman official, perhaps of Milesian origin, who had been prefect of Egypt and procurator of Asia. Characteristic of the baths is the extensive use, for piers, corners, vaults and domes, of cut stone and ashlar fitted together with metal clamps and used in conjunction with mortared rubble, which is also used for some of the domes. Owing to the nature of the local stone (river boulders and pebbles), much of the facing is extremely coarse.[37] In the Domitianic Nymphaeum and aqueduct, erected in honour of Trajan's father, the piers are built of mortared rubble faced with stones of varying sizes; the arches are turned with flat fieldstones set in thick mortar.[38] In the Humeitepe Baths, built around the turn of the century, the facing of the mortared rubble walls has become more regular, although corners and some lower wall sections still employ a lot of reused ashlar. There are traces of vaults built wholly or partly of radially set brick.[39] Again in the baths built by Faustina, wife of Marcus Aurelius, lower wall sections, door-frames, piers and arches have an ashlar facing of a concrete core, fitted together with dowels and clamps; and there are brick barrel vaults side by side with others of mortared rubble.[40] The second-century renovation of the theatre included huge retaining walls faced with a double layer of marble blocks masking a core of mortared rubble of excellent quality. Two annular corridors have vaults of rubble supported by a system of medium-sized voussoirs, set on walls of ashlar-faced concrete, their blocks joined by metal clamps.[41] Yet, with the exception of the Capito Baths, which had been trend-setting in many respects, the Roman architecture at Miletus was far less innovative than that of the other big cities of Asia.

The situation in the cities on the southern shore of the Propontis is less clear. At Nicaea a facing of ashlar masking a concrete core was used for the exterior walls and vaults of the Trajanic cavea of the theatre.[42] Much later, probably shortly after the middle of the third century, the towers of the city walls were built of brick-faced mortared rubble, a typical Italian technique. The curtain walls, however, have alternating bands of rubble masonry and brickwork running through the core.[43] In nearby Nicomedia very few Roman remains are preserved, but they include, among others, a large building at or near the water's edge, remarkable for the very tough quality of its concrete walls or foundations.[44]

Further to the south, most of the old centres in the interior of Caria continued to use ashlar or a combination of solid ashlar for the structural parts of a building with mortared rubble for the intervening sections.[45]

In neighbouring Lycia the new building techniques seem already to have been introduced before the region joined the Roman Empire under Claudius. In fact, a cenotaph erected at Limyra during the last decade of Augustus' reign, for his adoptive son Gaius Caesar, who died there, has a massive socle in rusticated ashlar masking a core of rubble set in an excellent mortared rubble, and supporting an enormous tower-shaped structure, whose facing of ashlar penetrated a concrete core. The monument may have been built by the Lycian League, with the agreement, if not according to the wishes, of Augustus himself.[46] The fact that the type of building is definitely Western and that its decoration includes a cymatium type characteristic of Rome, for which we have no other parallels in Asia Minor,[47] might even suggest the involvement of architects trained in the capital. Another 'Romanized' monument can be found at Myra, where, probably in the third century, baths were built of fired brick.[48] On the whole however, the Lycians maintained their tradition of good stoneworking right into the Byzantine period. Good second-century examples are the granaries at Patara and Andriake, where even polygonal walls occur.[49]

In the cities of Pamphylia a tradition of fine dressed masonry, going back to Pergamene domination, remained the basis of local building practices throughout antiquity. Whereas the materials were originally local stones, by the twenties of the second century these had been superseded by imported marble, which led to the development of the so-called 'Imperial marble style'. But even then dressed stone of local origin continued to be used almost everywhere for the walls and vaults that accompanied the fine marble detail.[50]

At Perge the Hellenistic ashlar tradition of the city walls reappears in several buildings of Imperial date, such as the Claudian Palaestra of Cornutus and the Hadrianic Nymphaeum.[51] The sloping barrel vaults of dressed, pitched stones carried by rusticated ashlar walls, supporting the seating of the second-century stadium, are among the best-preserved ashlar vaulted substructures in Asia Minor.[52] At Perge Roman influence only becomes tangible in the brick barrel vaults of some second-century baths and some later Roman structures on the agora.[53]

On the other hand, Side, although continuing to build ashlar monuments right into the third century, including the vaulted substructures of its second-century theatre,[54] seems to have been more responsive to Roman building techniques. Thus, lime mortar is used in the foundations of both second-century Harbour Temples, while in some late second-century structures ashlar faces a mortared rubble core,[55] and a second- or early third-century latrine in the agora has a typical barrel vault of mortared rubble faced with smaller stones.[56] Some third-century temples have a facing of ashlar orthostats around a concrete podium.[57] The enclosure of a late third-century ashlar temple in the West Necropolis consists of brick arches carried on ashlar piers, while the lower sections of its curtain walls are made of cemented fieldstones, though with upper sections of solid brick.[58]

Nearby Aspendus remained faithful to its Hellenistic ashlar tradition in most of its buildings dated to the first or second century. Yet, the new techniques make a remarkable appearance in some of its third-century monuments, such as the long basilica in the agora, carried by a double tier of vaulted substructures. Their vaulting, of brick laid in radial courses below, with the central portion pitched on their edges, a common device in many Early Byzantine buildings, is the most outstanding example of brick vaulting in Asia Minor, applying the structural principles of pitched mudbrick vaults from Egypt and Mesopotamia to fired bricks.[59] Yet, without any doubt, the most singular building at Aspendus is the aqueduct. Its bridge is carried on piers of mortared rubble faced with isodomic ashlar, solid stone also being used for the arches. The upper portions of the pressure towers, however, are built of mortared rubble faced with brick in the upper part of the tower and alternating bands of rubble and brick in the walls of the ramps. The upper arches had a double ring of brick voussoirs.[60]

Whereas the cities of Western Pamphylia thus continued using ashlar for most of their buildings, those of Eastern Pamphylia show a progressive adoption of the new building methods.

The region to the east, Cilicia, developed totally different building practices with a pronounced Italian character. To a great extent this must have been due to the presence of volcanic sand similar to that of Italy, which allowed the development of a mortar which had the almost monolithic strength of that used in the best Roman concrete.[61] The western part of Cilicia (Cilicia Aspera) had formed no cultural links with major centres before its contact with Rome and as a result may have been more susceptible to direct Roman influences once it was incorporated into the Roman Empire. The fact that there was for a long time a strong Roman military presence in the area may also have played a role in the adoption of typically Italian building methods. The ubiquitous building material here is a stout mortared rubble masonry of volcanic basalt, laid horizontally in mortar, roofed with barrel-vaults, half-domes and even full domes, constructed around an inner face of stones laid radially upon a wooden framework.[62]

In the central section of coastal Cilicia, east of Seleucia, direct Italian influence seems to be even stronger. At Corycus, for instance, the mortar used in the baths has the consistency and properties of Roman concrete, while the irregularly shaped facing stones resemble Roman *opus incertum*.[63] At nearby Elaeussa-Sebaste a bath building has concrete walls resembling Roman concrete in their texture, while the facing is of typically Italian *opus reticulatum*, alternating with brick bonding-courses. These, again in the Italian manner, are not set into the core to any significant extent.[64] The building technique used here can only be paralleled in Asia Minor in a so far unidentified and undated building at Paphlagonian Amastris and also in the city walls at Samosata.[65] At Elaeussa the harbour mole, again, is of excellent concrete.[66] Therefore it is the more remarkable that it is exactly this area which witnesses a strong revival of ashlar construction in its Early Byzantine religious architecture.[67]

In Plain Cilicia, near the Syrian border, several large late Roman buildings at the Roman foundation of Augusta and at Anazarbus have walls and vaults of excellent concrete, again faced in the Roman manner with bricks which do not run throughout the core.[68] They are the best examples of this technique in Asia Minor and could be connected with the almost permanent presence of the Roman army in the area during the later Empire.

In Pisidia, just north of Pamphylia, the building techniques of the Imperial period in cities with a rich Hellenistic past, such as Termessus, Sagalassus and Selge, remained faithful to the old ashlar tradition. A good example is the second- or third-century Gymnasium at Termessus, whose entire structure, including the vaults, is made of solid stone.[69] Only Selge betrays some Roman influence, for instance in the ashlar-faced concrete upper structure of the Eurymedon bridge.[70]

In Phrygia and Galatia the ashlar tradition again remained strong throughout the Imperial period. At the Augustan colony of Antioch most buildings are built of squared stone throughout. Only the probably early Imperial city walls and the second- or third-century baths are made of ashlar masonry around a core of mortared rubble.[71]

In the Hellenistic foundations of the Lycus and Maeander valleys, such as Laodicea and Hierapolis, most buildings maintained the ashlar tradition right to the end of the Empire, concrete faced with ashlar being confined to some walls exposed to the activity of water.[72]

At Aezani the second-century Temple of Zeus, including the single barrel-vaulted subterranean chamber which supported it, was built of solid stone. Mortared rubble only occurs as a filling of the immense podium into which the temple foundations were set. It also occurs, faced with ashlar slabs, in the upper structure of the local bridges, which had solid ashlar piers and arches. Two second-century bath buildings on the site use a framework of solid ashlar piers and curtain walls in the 'petit appareil' technique, to support brick arches and vaults.[73]

At Pessinus the adoption of Roman building techniques was very slow and apparently never became widespread. Although lime mortar used as a levelling device occurs in some first-century A.D. foundation courses of quay walls, mortared rubble makes its first appearance in the foundations of the probably second-century colonnades. In the early third century it also forms the core behind an ashlar-faced quay wall. But even then, clamps and dowels, rather than the quality of the mortar, guaranteed the stability of the structure.[74]

Galatian Ankara may have been more innovative. Whereas its Augustan sanctuary still has foundations which, like those of the sanctuary at Pessinus dated to the reign of Tiberius, are built of solid ashlar embedded in a mass of earth and rubble,[75] the baths erected during the reign of Caracalla are a thoroughly Western structure in building technique and other details. In fact the walls are built of a rubble fill with a facing of very carefully shaped smaller blocks, alternating with brick courses running through the thickness of the wall. Some of the smaller rooms may have been brick-vaulted.[76]

After this survey it ought to be clear that the translation of Roman concrete into local forms and the scale of its adoption were different in each region of Asia Minor, since they were determined both by local building techniques and by local materials. Mainly because of the poor quality of the mortar that was available, concrete in Asia Minor, with a few exceptions (mostly concentrated in Cilicia), never acquired the special architectural character and qualities of the fully developed Roman concrete, which was far more solid and homogeneous. This explains why in Asia Minor the facing always retained a stabilizing function and presented so many local varieties.

Mortared rubble seems to have been introduced towards the middle of the first century B.C. at Ephesus, where, in the Hellenistic tradition, it was originally faced with ashlar. 'Petit appareil' or related fieldstone facings became a common feature from the Augustan period onwards at Pergamum, and elsewhere from the middle of the first century A.D. Curtain walls in this technique, combined with ashlar or ashlar-faced rubble, taking the concentrated loads of vaults and arches, eventually became widespread, especially from the early second century onwards. Fired brick, gradually introduced during the first century, led to spectacular combinations of brick walls and vaults carried by ashlar in second-century Ephesus, and during the same century also appeared in more isolated solid brick buildings in other cities. Yet in Asia Minor, bricks usually run through the entire thickness of walls and vaults, which distinguishes them from the Italian technique of brick construction.[77] At the latest from the Antonine period onwards, concrete sections faced with fieldstones or small cut stones do also alternate with brick bonding-courses, again running through the complete rubble core. Typically Italian facings of *opus latericium* and *opus reticulatum* were mainly confined to Cilicia and some other isolated examples. An original contribution of Asia Minor was the introduction of pitched fired brick vaulting, actually an application of centuries-old Near Eastern mudbrick techniques to fired brick.

The wars and the misrule of Asia Minor during the Republican period cannot be held solely responsible for the introduction of Roman building techniques nearly two centuries after their first appearance in Italy. There were other equally decisive factors, such as, for instance, the plentiful supplies of fine building-stones and timber in many regions, which, together with the lingering role of a centuries-old tradition of excellent ashlar masonry, maintained these as the natural and most obvious materials for monumental architecture.[78] There is also the fact that the most obvious transmitters of techniques which had their roots in Italy, namely the late Republican governors and other Roman officials, do not seem to have been actively involved in whatever construction was going on at the time in the Asiatic provinces.[79] That such a personal involvement of people with explicit western connections may eventually have been the most decisive factor in the introduction of Roman concrete construction, at least in the initial phase of its application, is suggested by the fact that, as the examples at Ephesus[80] and Limyra show, the oldest concrete monuments all seem to have been erected by (or at least for) people of Western origin, even if their construction may have been carried out by local craftsmen. Its full-scale application at Sardis may have been the result of the supervision of the rebuilding of the city by an official sent from Rome. Again, it can hardly have been a mere coincidence that the first solid brick monument at Ephesus and the first major concrete building at Miletus were both creations of people who, as Roman officials, must have encountered

Roman building techniques elsewhere. The definitely Italian character of much of the construction in Cilicia may partly be connected with a strong Roman military presence in the area. Similar direct ties with Italy cannot be invoked, though, for the early use of 'petit appareil' at Pergamum. Perhaps the explanation here may be found both in the Hellenistic local experiments with lime mortar and in the fact that Pergamum, because of its political importance, had, more than any other city of the peninsula, been exposed for over two centuries to Roman influences.

Yet Asia Minor was not a mere recipient in the whole process. The Roman influences were absorbed, or sometimes even rejected, by the local traditions and given a new direction. When accepted, they sometimes resulted in an original blend of Roman and Hellenistic building practices, which, from the middle of the first century A.D. onwards, especially in the western coastal lands, began to transform the urban landscape. This repertory was inherited by the Byzantine architects, who eventually extended it throughout the Eastern Mediterranean.[81]

NOTES

* Research Associate of the National Fund for Scientific Research (Belgium).

[1] The best summaries thus far are: J. B. Ward-Perkins in D. Talbot-Rice (ed.), *The Great Palace of the Byzantine Emperors* (Edinburgh, 1958), 77–104; F. Fasolo, 'L'architettura romana di Efeso', *Bollettino del Centro di Studio per la Storia dell'Architettura*, xviii (1962), 7–91; R. L. Vann, 'A Study of Roman Construction in Asia Minor. The Lingering Role of a Hellenistic Tradition of Ashlar Masonry', dissertation, Cornell University, 1976, *passim*; J. B. Ward-Perkins, *Roman Imperial Architecture*, 2nd edn. (Harmondsworth, 1981), 273–8; H. Dodge, 'The use of brick in Asia Minor', *Yayla*, v (1984), 10–15, and see below, pp. 106–16.

[2] On those, see: Ward-Perkins, in Talbot-Rice, *op. cit.* (note 1), 57, 78–81, 95; Vann, *op. cit.* (note 1), 2, 9–11; C. Mango, *Byzantine Architecture* (New York, 1976), 14.

[3] Th. Wiegand, *Priene* (Berlin, 1904), 42; E. Boehringer and F. Krauss, *AvPerg*, ix (1937), 76; R. Martin, *Manuel d'architecture grecque*, i (Paris, 1965), 373; A. W. Lawrence, *Greek Aims in Fortification* (Oxford, 1979), 75–107, 209–11, 332; Vann, *op. cit.* (note 1), 62–3, 185. Compare also Plutarch, *Kimon*, 13; Vitruvius, ii.6.3; ii.8.5–9. For Asia Minor see also notes 7 (Pergamum) and 28 (Sardis).

[4] R. Stillwell, *Corinth*, i.2 (Cambridge, Mass., 1941), 31–49, pls. 5–7 (Upper Peirene). See also note 28 (Sardis).

[5] Compare Ward-Perkins in Talbot-Rice, *op. cit.* (note 1), 78; Vann, *op. cit.* (note 1), 19.

[6] See Ward-Perkins in Talbot-Rice, *op. cit.* (note 1), 95; Ward-Perkins, *op. cit.* (note 1), 273; A. Bammer, 'Ein Rundfries mit Bukranien und Girlanden', *JÖAI*, xlix (1968–71), 24–6; Vann, *op. cit.* (note 1), 10–11, 72–4, 169, 197; O. Ziegenaus and G. De Luca, *AvPerg*, xi.1 (1968), 71; W. Alzinger, 'Ephesos', *ANRW*, ii.7.2 (1980), 815; W. Alzinger, *Augusteische Architektur in Ephesos* (Vienna, 1974), 66, 147. On the differences between Roman concrete and its counterpart in Asia Minor, see: Ward-Perkins in Talbot-Rice, *op. cit.* (note 1), 82–3, 95; Vann, *op. cit.* (note 1), 9–11, 72–4, 169, 197; Ward-Perkins, *op. cit.* (note 1), 273, 274–6.

[7] cf. A. Conze, *AvPerg*, i.2 (1913), 154, 243–5; E. Boehringer and F. Krauss, *AvPerg*, ix (1937), 50–1, 76, pls. 6b, 24c, 33a–e, 42a, 72.

[8] W. Radt, 'Pergamon Vorbericht 1974', *TAD*, xiii.2 (1976), 81; *id.*, 'Pergamon. Vorbericht über die Kampagne 1975', *ibid.*, xxiv.1 (1977), 160–1. Cf. M. J. Mellink, 'Archaeology in Asia Minor', *AJA*, lxxviii (1974), 126, pl. 30, figs. 19–20.

[9] In the baths to the west of the big Upper Gymnasium, erected shortly before or around the middle of the first century, careful ashlar courses are still used in some walls, as well as in all supporting elements: P. Schazmann, *AvPerg*, vi (1923), 10, 82–4, fig. 26; Ward-Perkins in Talbot-Rice, *op. cit.* (note 1), 100. In the Asklepieion the new techniques do not even appear before the second half of the century: O. Ziegenaus and G. De Luca, *AvPerg*, xi.1 (1968), 71, 72, 74, 75, 88. In the Trajaneum the

foundations of temple and courtyard consist of a series of walls and barrel vaults, both in cut stone and in mortared rubble: H. Stiller, *AvPerg*, v.2 (1895), 5–14, 36, 38, 41, 43, 46, 49, pls. 2–9; Vann, *op. cit.* (note 1), 96–9, 107–9. In the early second-century amphitheatre the 'petit appareil' facing of the radial supporting walls gives way to ashlar near the outer extremities: Ward-Perkins in Talbot-Rice, *op. cit.* (note 1), 83, 100, pl. 27B.

[10] Schazmann, *op. cit.* (note 9), 16, 61, 84–5; Ward-Perkins in Talbot-Rice, *op. cit.* (note 1), 84, 100, pl. 27D–E.

[11] Ward-Perkins in Talbot-Rice, *op. cit.* (note 1), 89; O. Ziegenaus and G. De Luca, *AvPerg*, xi.3 (1981), 31–7, 46, 68–9. The temple itself was built by the Pergamene consul L. Cuspius Rufinus. See Ch. Hubicht, *AvPerg*, viii.3 (1969), 9–14.

[12] Ward-Perkins in Talbot-Rice, *op. cit.* (note 1), 84, 100, pl. 27C; Vann, *op. cit.* (note 1), 88–92; Ward-Perkins, *op. cit.* (note 1), 283–5; Ziegenaus and De Luca, *op. cit.* (note 11), 76–80, 83, 86–7, 95, 98–9, pls. 26a–b, 27b, 28b, 78–9, 83.

[13] Ward-Perkins in Talbot-Rice, *op. cit.* (note 1), 85, 100, pl. 30; O. Deubner, 'Das Heiligtum der alexandrinischen Gottheiten in Pergamon genannt "Kizil Avli" ("Rote Halle")', *Istanbuler Mitteilungen*, xxvii–xxviii (1977–8), 230–40, 248, pls. 58–72.

[14] W. Radt, 'Pergamon. Vorbericht über die Kampagne 1976', *TAD*, xxv.1 (1980), 236, 245.

[15] G. Niemann, *FiE*, i (1906), 144–5; Alzinger 1974 (*op. cit.*, note 6), 38, 40: *id.*, 'Ephesos', *ANRW*, ii.7.2 (1980), 812–14.

[16] Cf. E. Fossel, 'Zum Tempel auf dem Staatsmarkt in Ephesos', *JÖAI*, l (1972–5), 212–14, figs. 1–3, 5–7; W. Alzinger, 'Das Regierungsviertel', *JÖAI*, l (1972–5), Beibl., 283–4, 287–93; *id.*, 'Ephesos', *ANRW*, ii.7.2 (1980), 814. For a different opinion about date or identification, see W. Jobst, 'Zur Lokalisierung des Sebasteion-Augusteum in Ephesos', *Istanbuler Mitteilungen*, xxx (1980), 246 ff. (Sebasteion); K. Tuchelt, 'Zum Problem, Kaisareion-Sebasteion', *ibid.*, xxxi (1981), 180 (Augustan).

[17] Alzinger 1972–5 (*op. cit.*, note 16), Beibl., 249–51; *id.* 1974 (*op. cit.*, note 6), 55–56; *id.*, 'Ephesos', *ANRW*, ii.7.2 (1980), 815–16.

[18] Alzinger 1974 (*op. cit.*, note 6), 42–3.

[19] A. Bammer, 'Die politische Symbolik des Memmiusbaues', *JÖAI*, l (1972–5), 220, 222; Alzinger 1974 (*op. cit.*, note 6), 16–19.

[20] W. Wilberg, *FiE*, iii (1923), 256–62, figs. 263–6, 269, 270; Alzinger 1974 (*op. cit.*, note 6), 22–3; *id.*, 'Ephesos', *ANRW*, ii.7.2 (1980), 817.

[21] On these monuments, see: A. Bammer, 'Das Denkmal des C. Sextilius Pollio in Ephesos', *JÖAI*, li (1976–7), Beibl., 81–2, figs. 2–3; 86, 89, 92; Alzinger 1974 (*op. cit.* note 6), 28–9, 65; *id.*, 'Ephesos', *ANRW*, ii.7.2 (1980), 817.

[22] See on both buildings: R. Herberdey, G. Niemann and W. Wilberg, *FiE*, ii (1912), 35, figs. 64, 68, 72; Ward-Perkins in Talbot-Rice, *op. cit.* (note 1), 84, 98, pl. 29B–C; Fasolo, *op. cit.* (note 1), 27; Vann, *op. cit.* (note 1), 103, 117.

[23] H. Vetters, 'Domitianterrasse und Domitiangasse', *JÖAI*, l (1972–5), Beibl., 313–15, figs. 6–7.

[24] C. Praschniker, *FiE*, v.1 (1953), 35–6, 41, figs. 73–5; Ward-Perkins in Talbot-Rice, *op. cit.* (note 1), 85, 97; W. Alzinger, 'Ephesos', *ANRW*, ii.7.2 (1980), 822; Ward-Perkins, *op. cit.* (note 1), 288–90, fig. 187; Dodge, *op. cit.* (note 1), 13. V. M. Strocka recently informed me of an older example in a Vespasianic bath building at Lycian Patara.

[25] Ward-Perkins in Talbot-Rice, *op. cit.* (note 1), 85, 97; Fasolo, *op. cit.* (note 1), 29–53; W. Alzinger, 'Ephesos', *ANRW*, ii.7.2 (1980), 821, 823; Dodge, *op. cit.* (note 1), 13, fig. 7.

[26] Ward-Perkins in Talbot-Rice, *op. cit.* (note 1), 97, pls. 26A–D; Fasolo, *op. cit.* (note 1), 43–4, 53, figs. 26, 31, 35, 38.

[27] W. Alzinger, 'Ephesos', *ANRW*, ii.7.2 (1980), 823.

[28] G. M. A. Hanfmann and J. C. Waldbaum, *A Survey of Sardis and the Major Monuments outside the City Walls* (Cambridge and London, 1975), 79; G. M. A. Hanfmann, *Sardis from Prehistoric to Roman Times* (Cambridge, 1983), 59, 118, 124, 170, 207, 263 n. 50.

[29] Hanfmann and Waldbaum, *op. cit.* (note 28), 31; Hanfmann, *op. cit.* (note 28), 141–2.

[30] Vann, *op. cit.* (note 1), 99–103; Hanfmann, *op. cit.* (note 28), 118, 142, 263 n. 51.

[31] Hanfmann and Waldbaum, *op. cit.* (note 28), 108–9.

[32] Vann, *op. cit.* (note 1), 143, 154; Hanfmann, *op. cit.* (note 28), 142–3; F. Yeğül in Hanfmann, *op. cit.* (note 28), 160, fig. 218.

[33] Hanfmann, *op. cit.* (note 28), 142–3, 145; F. Yeğül in Hanfmann, *op. cit.* (note 28), 153–4, 160, figs. 212, 214, 216, 219, 233.

[34] Vann, *op. cit.* (note 1), 143, 159, 168; Hanfmann and Waldbaum, *op. cit.* (note 28), 139–40, 151, 165, 187 n. 16; Hanfmann, *op. cit.* (note 28), 142.

[35] A. von Gerkan, *Milet*, i.6 (Berlin and Leipzig, 1922), 56–7, 72; G. Kleiner, *Das römische Milet* (Wiesbaden, 1970), 121 f., fig. 1; W. Alzinger, 'Ephesos', *ANRW*, ii.7.2 (1980), 813.

[36] Von Gerkan, *op. cit.* (note 35), 44–7, 96–7; K. Tuchelt, 'Buleuterion und Ara Augusti', *Istanbuler Mitteilungen*, xxv (1975), 120–1, 136.

[37] A. von Gerkan and F. Krischen, *Milet*, i.9 (Berlin and Leipzig, 1938), 23, 32, 36, 37, 44–5, figs. 43–6; Ward-Perkins in Talbot-Rice, *op. cit.* (note 1), 99, pl. 28c–d; *id.*, *op. cit.* (note 1), 295–6.

[38] J. Hülsen, *Milet*, i.5 (Berlin and Leipzig, 1949), 4–5; Ward-Perkins in Talbot-Rice, *op. cit.* (note 1), 99, pl. 28e; Vann, *op. cit.* (note 1), 85.

[39] A. von Gerkan in von Gerkan and Krischen, *op. cit.* (note 37), 127–8, 130–1, 141, pls. 38–9; Ward-Perkins in Talbot-Rice, *op. cit.* (note 1), 99, pl. 27a.

[40] F. Krischen in von Gerkan and Krischen, *op. cit.* (note 37), 55, 59, 60, 74–5, 85, figs. 72, 74, 84, 101–5, 111–12; Ward-Perkins in Talbot-Rice, *op. cit.* (note 1), 84, pls. 26e, 28b; Vann, *op. cit.* (note 1), 154.

[41] F. Krauss, *Milet*, iv.1 (Berlin, 1973), 65–6, 77; Vann, *op. cit.* (note 1), 103, 113.

[42] B. Yalman, 'İznik Tiyatro Kazısı 1982', *V. Kazı sonuçları toplantısı* (Istanbul, 1983), 215–20, figs. 1–2. Cf. Pliny, *Ep. ad Traj.* 39.

[43] Ward-Perkins in Talbot-Rice, *op. cit.* (note 1), 86, 99, pl. 31b–d; Vann, *op. cit.* (note 1), 80; Ward-Perkins, *op. cit.* (note 1), 277–8.

[44] Ward-Perkins in Talbot-Rice, *op. cit.* (note 1), 100.

[45] See, for instance, the baths at Alabanda: Edhem Bey, 'Fouilles d'Alabanda en Carie', *Comptes rendus de l'Académie des Inscriptions et Belles Lettres*, ii (1905), pl. ii; the baths at Aphrodisias: L. Crema, 'I monumenti architettonici afrodisiensi', *Monumenti antichi*, xxxviii (1939), 264, 269–70, fig. 39; Ward-Perkins, *op. cit.* (note 1), 296. For solid ashlar construction in Caria, see, for instance: M. Anabolu, 'Alinda Karpuzlu', *TAD*, xiv.1–2 (1962), 94, figs. 5–8; G. E. Bean, *Turkey beyond the Maeander* (London, 1971), 187, pl. 45; 197–8, pl. 51; Vann, *op. cit.* (note 1), 86.

[46] J. Borchhardt, 'Ein Kenotaph für Gaius Caesar', *JDAI*, lxxxix (1974), 221–41.

[47] J. Borchhardt, 'Limyra. Bericht über die Abschlusskampagne 1974', *TAD*, xxiv.1 (1977), 105 fig. 21.

[48] J. Borchhardt (ed.), *Myra*, Istanbuler Forschungen, xxx (Berlin, 1975), 61, fig. 10, pls. 28b, 29 a–c; Dodge, *op. cit.* (note 1), 10, fig. 5.

[49] Vann, *op. cit.* (note 1), 94, 124; Borchhardt, *op. cit.* (note 48), 65–7, 73, pls. 34, 36a–c, 44–5. For Byzantine examples, see R. M. Harrison, 'Lycia in Late Antiquity', *Yayla*, i (1977), 11, 14, figs. 4–5.

[50] See Ward-Perkins, *op. cit.* (note 1), 299–300.

[51] K. Lanckoronski, *Städte Pamphyliens und Pisidiens*, i: *Pamphylien* (Vienna, 1890), 42–4, figs. 31–2; Vann, *op. cit.* (note 1), 118–21; A. M. Mansel, '1971 Perge kazısı', *TAD*, xx.2 (1973), 144–5, 150–3, figs. 7–12.

[52] Lanckoronski, *op. cit.* (note 51), 55, 57, figs. 40–2; Vann, *op. cit.* (note 1), 114–17.

[53] Ward-Perkins in Talbot-Rice, *op. cit.* (note 1), 101; M. J. Mellink, 'Archaeology in Asia Minor', *AJA*, lxxviii (1974), 117.

[54] Vann, *op. cit.* (note 1), 110–13; A. M. Mansel, *Die Ruinen von Side* (Berlin, 1963), 122–4, figs. 105, 107, 109.

[55] *Ibid.*, 36, 77, 81.

[56] Vann, *op. cit.* (note 1), 160.

[57] *Ibid.*, 104–7; Mansel, *op. cit.* (note 54), 86–7, 102–7.

[58] *Ibid.*, 177, 182, 184–5, 186–7, figs. 145, 147, 151.

[59] Ward-Perkins in Talbot-Rice, *op. cit.* (note 1), 90–5, 96, pl. 32; Dodge, *op. cit.* (note 1), 13, fig. 10. An example dated c. A.D. 90–100 occurs in an Egyptianizing building at Argos: see P. Aubert, *Comptes rendus de l'Académie des Inscriptions et Belles Lettres* (1985), 169. Much later the same technique is still used in the fortress at Harran.

[60] J. B. Ward-Perkins, 'The aqueduct of Aspendos', *PBSR*, xxiii (1955), 115–23; *id.* in Talbot-Rice, *op. cit.* (note 1), 86, 96, pl. 31e; Vann, *op. cit.* (note 1), 80–5; Ward-Perkins, *op. cit.* (note 1), 303.

[61] Ward-Perkins in Talbot-Rice, *op. cit.* (note 1), 82; Ward-Perkins, *op. cit.* (note 1), 275.

[62] G. Huber, 'Vorläufige Beobachtungen über die Städteplanung in den Küstenorten des westlichsten Kilikien', *TAD*, xiii.2 (1964), 140; E. Rosenbaum, G. Huber and S. Onurkan, *A Survey of Coastal Cities in Western Cilicia* (Ankara, 1967), 3–4, 8, 70, 74; J. Russell, 'Anemurium: the changing face of a Roman city', *Archaeology*, xxxiii (1980), 33; Ward-Perkins, *op. cit.* (note 1), 304–5.

[63] Ward-Perkins in Talbot-Rice, *op. cit.* (note 1), 82, 98, pl. 24A–B.

[64] J. Keil and A. Wilheem, *MAMA*, iii (1931), 222, fig. 178, pl. 56, 177; Ward-Perkins in Talbot-Rice, *op. cit.* (note 1), 82, 96, pl. 25A–D; Rosenbaum *et al.*, *op. cit.* (note 62), 74; Dodge, *op. cit.* (note 1), 10, fig. 2.

[65] For Amastris, see S. Eyice, 'Deux anciennes églises byzantines de la citadelle d'Amasra (Paphlagonie)', *Cahiers archéologiques*, vii (1954), 100, pl. XXXVIII, 1. We owe the reference to Samosata to Dr David French. These walls will be published shortly by A. A. Tırpan.

[66] Ward-Perkins in Talbot-Rice, *op. cit.* (note 1), 82.

[67] S. Guyer and E. Herzfeld, *MAMA*, ii (1930), 10–11, figs. 1, 8; 62–7, fig. 64; Keil and Wilhelm, *op. cit.* (note 64), 36–8, pls. 18, 19, 20, 61, 91–9, figs. 109–10, 112–14, 123, 132–43, 145; M. Gough, 'Excavations at Alahan 1967', *TAD*, xvi.1 (1967), 95–9; *id.*, 'Alahan Monastery 1968', *TAD*, xvii.1 (1968), 67–70; S. Hill, 'Dağ Pazarı and its monuments', *Yayla*, ii (1979), 11, fig. 5; R. M. Harrison, 'The monastery on Mahras Dağ in Isauria', *Yayla*, iii (1980), 24, figs. 2–3.

[68] See, for Augusta: M. Akok, 'Augusta şehri harabesi', *TAD*, vii.2 (1957), 17–20, pls. XI–XXII; M. Gough, 'Augusta Cilicia', *AS*, vi (1956), 173 ff., pls. XVa–b, XVIa; Rosenbaum *et al.*, *op. cit.* (note 62), 77. For Anazarbus, see M. Gough, 'Anazarbus', *AS*, ii (1952), 105–6; P. Verzone, 'Città ellenistiche e romane dell'Asia Minore. Anazarbus', *Palladio*, vii (1957), 22, and my own observations in 1985.

[69] K. Lanckoronski, *Städte Pamphyliens und Pisidiens*, ii: *Pisidien* (Vienna, 1892), 60, 103–4; Vann, *op. cit.* (note 1), 124.

[70] Vann, *op. cit.* (note 1), 87. For the other buildings, see: A. Machatschek and M. Schwarz, *Bauforschungen in Selge* (Vienna, 1981), 66, 87 n. 575; 109.

[71] Cf. Ward-Perkins, *op. cit.* (note 1), 280. A monograph on Antioch by S. Mitchell and the writer is in preparation.

[72] For instance, G. Weber, 'Die Hochdruck-Wasserleitung von Laodicea ad Lycum', *JDAI*, xiii (1898), 2–4, figs. 2–4; 7–9, fig. 13; 10, fig. 14; G. Weber, 'Wasserleitungen in kleinasiatischen Städten', *JDAI*, xix (1904), 94. On the ashlar tradition, see: P. Verzone, 'Le chiese di Hierapolis', *Cahiers archéologiques*, viii (1956), 40, 42, figs. 2–8; 45, figs. 9–12; 54–6, figs. 17–28; 56–9; Vann, *op. cit.* (note 1), 77, 94, 159, 168; Ward-Perkins, *op. cit.* (note 1), 273.

[73] See Vann, *op. cit.* (note 1), 86, 109; R. Naumann, *Der Zeustempel zu Aizanoi* (Berlin, 1979), 13, 16 fig. 7; R. Naumann, 'Aizanoi. Bericht über die Ausgrabungen und Untersuchungen 1978', *AA*, 1980, 126–30; *id.*, 'Aizanoi. Bericht über die Ausgrabungen und Untersuchungen 1979 und 1980', *AA*, 1982, 345–7, 371; *id.*, 'Die Grabungen bei der römischen Thermenanlage', *TAD*, xxv.2 (1980), 168–72.

[74] See M. Waelkens in J. Devreker and M. Waelkens, *Les Fouilles de la Rijksuniversiteit te Gent à Pessinonte 1967–1973*, Dissertationes Archaeologicae Gandenses, xxii (Brugge, 1984), 88–90, 107, 115–16, 122–3, 137, 139–40, 141. On the temple at Pessinus, see now M. Waelkens, 'The Imperial Sanctuary at Pessinus', *Epigraphica Anatolica*, vii (1986), 37–73.

[75] See D. Krencker and M. Schede, *Der Tempel in Ankara* (Berlin and Leipzig, 1936), 23–6, 28, 30, figs. 26, 28, 30.

[76] M. Akok, 'Ankara şehrindeki Roma hamamı', *TAD*, xvii.1 (1968), 5–37, figs. 11–13, 16, 17, 22; Vann, *op. cit.* (note 1), 130; Ward-Perkins, *op. cit.* (note 1), 279–80.

[77] See Ward-Perkins in Talbot-Rice, *op. cit.* (note 1), 85; Dodge, *op. cit.* (note 1), 10, 13.

[78] Vann, *op. cit.* (note 1), 2, 6, 64, 71, 173, 191; Ward-Perkins, *op. cit.* (note 1), 273.

[79] See K. Tuchelt, *Frühe Denkmäler Roms in Kleinasien*, Istanbuler Mitteilungen, Beiheft 23 (Tübingen, 1979), 127–9.

[80] Cf. also Alzinger 1974 (*op. cit.*, note 6), 150–1.

[81] Cf. Ch. Delvoye, 'Sur le passage des voûtes et des coupoles en briques de l'Anatolie à la péninsule balkanique', *BCH*, c (1976), 235–8; Mango, *op. cit.* (note 2), 9, 11, 14; Ward-Perkins in Talbot-Rice, *op. cit.* (note 1), 75–95, 101–4.

Brick Construction in Roman Greece and Asia Minor[1]

Hazel Dodge

The first major public monument in Rome to make substantial use of fired brick was the Tiberian Castra Praetoria. This was built entirely of brick-faced concrete.[2] From the time of Nero the use of fired brick in Rome and Italy as a facing material for *opus caementicium* was the convention. The brick facing served no structural purpose, though during construction it did act as shuttering for the concrete core. From the time of Domitian *bipedales*, bricks 2 feet square, were used. These were laid in a single course, often going right through the wall.[3] This gave stability to the wall as the core settled, but the main function of such a course of *bipedales* was to mark the end of a section of work. Vaulting in Rome and Italy was always carried out in *opus caementicium*.

The brick facing, however, has acquired an important function in modern research, that of chronological indicator. It has been noticed, and proved, that the mortar joints between the bricks become thicker over time (table 1), although the thickness of the bricks is only fractionally less in the fourth and fifth centuries than in the Augustan period. It would be of great interest and of enormous value if such a phenomenon could be shown to have occurred in Greece and Asia Minor.[4]

Compared with Rome and Italy, the provinces exhibit more variation in the use of materials and therefore to a certain extent in the techniques as well. This is particularly evident in the eastern provinces, where a number of traditions, apart from that of Rome, were at work. In Greece and Asia Minor the architectural traditions owed much to the Classical Greek and Hellenistic periods.

Fired brick was used as a building material from the third millennium B.C., for example in the Sumerian cities, and from the sixth century B.C. at Babylon for walls and vaults.[5] Brick in general was not a material favoured by the Classical Greeks, though a rare example survives at Olynthus dating to the fourth century B.C.[6] From the same period date the Thracian painted tombs which demonstrate a well-established tradition of wall and vault construction in brick.[7] The Parthians from the mid-third century B.C. made some use of fired brick for construction, though

TABLE I

(cm.)	Rome		Greece		Asia Minor	
	Brick thickness	Joint thickness	Brick thickness	Joint thickness	Brick thickness	Joint thickness
Augustus	3·5–4·2	Close	3		4·0–5·0	
Tiberius–Claudius	3·5–4·5	1·5	4·3–4·6	2		
Nero	3·9–4·5	0·5–1·5	4·0–4·5	0·5–2·0		
Domitian	3·6–4·2	0·5–2·0	4	1·5–2·0	4	2·75
Trajan	3·3–4·0	0·5–1·6	4·5	4	4	3·5
Hadrian	3·4–4·0	0·5–1·5	3·0–4·5	1·2–2·5	3·5–5·0	1·5–2·5
Antonine	3·4–4·0	0·5–1·8	3·0–4·0	2·0–3·0	4	1·5–2·0
Septimius Severus and Caracalla	3	0·5–2·5			3·5–5·5	4
3rd century	2·5–3·5	1·0–3·0	2·5–3·2	2·0	4·5	2·5
4th century	av. 3·5	1·5–3·5	2·5	2·5	4·0–5·0	3·5
5th century	2·5–3·2	1·5–3·5	2·5–3·0	3·3–4·0	4·5	3·5
6th century			2·3	3·5–5·0	4·25	5·5

mudbrick was more common because of its low cost and ease of manufacture.[8] It was not until the Roman period, however, that fired brick was extensively used in the eastern provinces, and then it was as a structural material in its own right, in contrast to the practice in Rome itself.

Nevertheless, some of the earliest uses of fired brick in both Greece and Asia Minor owe more to the metropolitan traditions. At Elaeussa-Sebaste in Cilicia, the Reticulate Baths were constructed of a material very similar to *opus caementicium* and faced with true *opus mixtum*, that is panels of reticulate masonry and brick.[9] As in metropolitan use, the sole purpose of the brickwork at Elaeussa was to give stability to the reticulate facing, penetrating into it but not often running through the core. In later examples in Greece and Asia Minor the situation is rather different. The context of the Reticulate Baths makes it reasonably certain that this use was directly inspired by Roman practice. Similarly, this may be the case at Sparta with the Roman stoa, dated to the reign of Augustus, which was of brick-faced mortared rubble.[10] This comprised a series of small compartments covered with barrel vaults, ten on either side of three large semi-circular niches at the back. All vaulting was in brick. A comparable brick vault, of the early first century A.D., is over Tomb 2 in the Artemis Sanctuary at Sardis (pl. X*a*).[11] The practice of using brick as a facing material was still quite common in Greece in the late Hadrianic period. At Buthrotum in modern Albania the mid-second-century nymphaeum was built of a mortared rubble core and faced with bricks of varying sizes,[12] and in the Antonine Baths at Sparta the mortared rubble core of the walls was faced with triangular bricks.[13] In Crete also, brick as a facing material was favoured in the Trajanic and Hadrianic periods, for example in the odeion and amphitheatre at Gortyna.[14]

By contrast, in Asia Minor brick appears at only two sites as a facing material, in addition to the instance at Elaeussa-Sebaste. At Augusta Ciliciae, where the buildings were not dated by the surveyors of the site more precisely than 'Roman', brick was used as a facing for a material judged to be of very similar character to Roman *opus caementicium*.[15] In the late fourth/early fifth century a building, possibly a bath complex, was constructed at Myra in Lycia (pl. IX), and, although brick was used only to face the walls, it was used for some of the vaulting.[16]

Solid brick construction

This type of construction became common in Roman Greece and Asia Minor, and may be seen as a local adaptation of a metropolitan material. The example *par excellence* of brick construction in the eastern provinces is the Kızıl Avlu at Pergamum, which was a Serapaeum, to judge from the finds of Egyptian sculpture and decoration. This has been variously dated to the reign of Hadrian and to the end of the second/beginning of the third century A.D. The walls were built of coursed mortared brick, partly whole and partly broken, brought to a face with whole bricks, about 23 cm. square and 30 cm. square.[17] In appearance this does bear a remarkable resemblance to Roman brickwork, which is accentuated by the use of bricks 52 cm. square in one part over a drain. This size may be seen as a local equivalent of the Roman *bipedalis*.

Elsewhere in Asia Minor brick was used in this way at Ephesus, Tralles and Aspendus. In Greece, examples occur at Athens, Argos, Isthmia, Cenchreae and Olympia.[18] Indeed on present evidence, wall, as opposed to vault, construction entirely in brick is more common in Greece than in Asia Minor. Why this should be so is too complex a question to be dealt with here.[19]

Alternate brick and stonework bands

The bands were generally of mortared rubble faced with small squared blocks and were levelled off by brick bonding-courses of a varying number of bricks, usually four to six. These bands of brickwork ran right through the core, and provided lateral cohesion for the wall core and facing, and prevented settlement. This kind of construction does not occur in the West until the second century A.D. at the earliest.[20] It is often claimed that it was a characteristically Asiatic technique,[21] but it was in widespread use in Greece, the Balkans and Asia Minor from an early date in the Roman period. The technique certainly gained favour in the late Roman and early Byzantine period in Constantinople and other major centres in Asia Minor, but in the earlier period it was not as common there as in Greece and the Balkans. In Greece examples include the Antonine aqueduct to the nymphaeum in the Agora at Athens, the mid-second-century odeion at Epidaurus, where the outer walls were built of bands of rubblework, about 30 cm. high, with a varying number of brick courses, and various examples at Argos.[22] In the Balkans, where, as it has already been seen, there thrived a brick-building tradition from the fourth century B.C., the mid-second-century A.D. Great Baths at Odessus, the second-century A.D. city walls of Serdica and the Severan warehouse at Tomis all extensively employed this type of wall construction.[23] In Asia Minor this technique was used at Sardis for the baths-gymnasium complex from the mid- to late second century A.D., and for the Caracallan Baths at Ankara, as well as for the third-century walls at Nicaea.[24] From the Tetrarchic period this method of wall construction became typical in Greece and Asia Minor and in the power centres elsewhere in the Empire—in, for example, the walls and buildings of Thessalonica (pl. X*b*), the walls of Constantinople, and, in the West,

PLATE IX

Myra: late fourth-/early fifth-century A.D. brick-faced building

PLATE X

a. Tomb 2, Sanctuary of the Temple of Artemis at Sardis

b. Brick bands in the construction of the Palace at Thessalonica

PLATE XI

a. Houses on the slopes of Bülbüldağ, Ephesus. Note the crown of the vault, which is of pitched brick

b. Detail of one of a series of pitched brick vaults beneath the North Basilica at Izmir

the Kaiserthermen at Trier.[25] The technique continued in use in the Balkans into the Byzantine period, for example at Hisar.[26] In Syria it occurs in a late Roman tomb at Apamea,[27] but then not until the time of Theodosius II, when the walls of Antioch on the Orontes were constructed in a fashion comparable with the walls of Constantinople. In the sixth century the technique occurs in the church and palace at Qasr ibn Warden.[28]

This type of construction is frequently misnamed *opus mixtum*, a term more properly applied to the Roman technique of brick and reticulate masonry facing a homogeneous concrete core. Thus it is not employed here.

Roman bricks varied in size and shape, but in Roman Greece and Asia Minor the bricks in normal use were roughly square or oblong, for example in the Vedius Gymnasium at Ephesus, 29–30 cm. square;[29] at Sparta, 27 cm. square;[30] at Eleusis, 40–42 cm. by 30–34 cm.;[31] and at Augusta Ciliciae, 42 by 35 cm.[32] In Asia Minor the square bricks averaged 30–35 cm. square, equivalent to the *pedalis* of western Roman use.[33] Oblong bricks, which are common at Olympia and Eleusis[34] and which seem to be less frequently used in Asia Minor, are not mentioned by Vitruvius. An equivalent of the Roman *bipedalis* was also used, for example at Argos in the Theatre Baths (56–58 cm. square), and at Pergamum in the Kızıl Avlu (52 cm. square).[35]

Square bricks were often cut into two or more triangles. In Rome, triangular bricks occur from the reign of Claudius.[36] This practice was quite common in Greece at Argos, Olympia and Sparta.[37] In Asia Minor, so far as is known, it does not occur.

The methods of dating Roman brickwork have attracted much attention from scholars. It has been generally accepted that the increasing thickness of the mortar joints with time is an important dating criterion for the brickwork of the capital. This can be roughly summarized as follows:

TABLE 2

Claudius to Domitian	2 joints	Thickness of 1 brick
Hadrian	3 joints	Thickness of 2 bricks
Septimius Severus	4 joints	Thickness of 3 bricks
Maxentius	1 joint	Thickness of 1 brick[38]

Lugli's figures show that as mortar joints increased in thickness, so bricks decreased, though at a lesser rate.[39] It was not a steady progression, and it is only a general scheme. Nevertheless, it would be of great value if such a scheme could be devised for the Eastern Mediterranean and of great interest if it were to follow that of Rome.

With reference to the measurements in table 1,[40] in Greece, although the diminution in the thickness of the bricks and the increase in the mortar joints is irregular, it is quite clear that by the fourth century A.D. the ratio of mortar joint to brick thickness was approximately 1:1, and by the fifth century the mortar joints were almost twice the thickness of the bricks. On some Greek sites in later periods there is a clear increase in the thickness of bricks between the fifth and sixth centuries, for instance at Philippi. In Basilica A (*c.* A.D. 500) the brick bands are of bricks 3 cm. thick separated by joints of about the same thickness. In Basilica B (*c.* sixth century A.D.) the bricks are 4–4·5 cm. thick separated by mortar beds 5–6·5 cm. thick. In Asia Minor a contemporary example is the Basilica of St John at Ephesus, where the bricks are 4–4·5 cm. thick and the joints only 3–3·5 cm., slightly below the average.[41] Generally the brick thicknesses in Asia Minor remain remarkably consistent and are on the whole greater than those used in Rome. The mortar joint thicknesses display a considerable amount of irregularity and variation which may, of course, be due to the scarcity of the available statistics. However, there does seem to be a general increase in the sixth century, when the proportion of brick to mortar is approximately 1:1; this occurs two centuries earlier in Greece and Rome. Thus it would seem that Greece shows a trend similar to that occurring in Rome, but in Asia Minor only the mortar joint thickness may be taken as a possible chronological indicator, and then only in a very general way.

Another feature which may be used for dating is the use of *bipedales* (or the local equivalent) as a bonding consisting of only one course of bricks passing through the core each time. In Italy bonding courses of *bipedales* at 3 to 4 ft. intervals are characteristic of the Domitianic period, and they are found again at 4 to 6 ft. intervals under Septimius Severus.[42] Such a technique occurs at Argos in the eastern part of the Theatre Baths, where the bonding course is made up of one course of square bricks, 56–58 cm. square, and 6·5–7 cm. thick, twice the thickness of those used in Rome, and occurring at about every 92–95 cm. This part of the baths was dated by Ginouvès to the late first century on the strength of this. Similar bricks also occur in the Hadrianic aqueduct at Argos, where they were used at the top of the pillars as the springing for the arches. These are about 60 cm. square, but only half as thick as those used in the baths.[43]

The existence in the East of large, imperially owned brickyards, characteristic of Italy, is doubtful. No brick-stamps have been identified in Greece or Asia Minor, apart from those of Herodes Atticus, and there appears to be little evidence for a centrally organized brick manufacturing industry. This particular area of study, however, has received little attention.[44]

Whereas the use of brick for wall construction may have been influenced by metropolitan practices, the use of brick for vaulting in Greece, and in particular in Asia Minor, was not. This technique came about through the lack of adequate materials to make *opus caementicium*, the vaulting medium *par excellence* of Rome. Other materials had to be exploited if the architects of the East were to have a vaulting medium that was as versatile, economical and of comparable strength. Brick was only one of the materials deployed, but it became the most important in the later period.

Ward-Perkins suggests two possible channels through which brick as a vaulting medium might first have passed into the architecture of western Asia Minor in the late first and early second centuries A.D. Firstly, Thrace and the Balkans:[45] here there are several examples, notably Hellenistic tombs, and the small second-century A.D. covered theatre at Nicopolis ad Istrum, where the stone seats were carried on brick vaults. These vaults are all of radially laid bricks and this is the normal technique in Greece and Asia Minor. Alternatively, the source might have been Syria, and here the case is harder to prove.[46] Fired brick was certainly used at Babylon in the sixth century B.C, but there is only a small amount of evidence for fired brick in Syria from the second century B.C. to the first century A.D. At Assur in the first-century A.D. palace, vaulting in fired brick occurs with the bricks laid, not radially, but pitched on end.[47] Pitched, fired brick vaulting occurs from the first century A.D. in Greece, but is more frequent in Asia Minor from the late second and early third centuries. There is no precedent for this type of vaulting in the architecture of the Roman West, of Greece, or of Asia Minor, but the structural principles behind this method had long been known and used in mudbrick construction in Mesopotamia and Egypt.[48] The earliest known examples of the technique in mudbrick appear to be in the third millennium B.C. at Saqqara in Egypt. Pitched brick vaulting in fired brick occurred at Assur and Seleucia on the Tigris from the early first century A.D.; possibly these examples influenced the implementation of the technique at Dura Europus.[49] In Egypt, the two sites of Karanis and Socnopaei Nesus afford the only surviving instances of pitched mudbrick vaulting in the Roman Empire; these date from the first century to the sixth century A.D.[50] The examples in fired brick in the Roman East are evidently a translation of this into a more durable material. The earliest instance appears to be in the oldest phase of the baths at Argos. At Eleusis a vault in a second-century aqueduct consisted of three curved bricks set on end.[51] In Asia Minor the earliest pitched brick vaulting occurs at Izmir in the substructures of the North Basilica in the agora (pl. XI*b*). This was presumably part of the later second-century rebuilding after an earthquake devastated the city.[52] The best-known example is in the substructures of the basilica at Aspendus (third century A.D.). Brick barrel vaults spring from a projecting course of large stone blocks on side walls of mortared rubble. The first eighteen to twenty-two courses are laid radially along either side, but the crown consists of bricks pitched across the line of the vault. A similar example occurs at Rhodiapolis in Lycia.[53] Pitched brick vaulting occurs in Tetrarchic Thessalonica, in the houses on the slopes of Bülbüldağ at Ephesus (pl. XI*a*), and in the late Roman cistern (?) on the slopes of the Acropolis at Athens.[54] In the Early Byzantine period pitched brick vaulting became very common at Constantinople, for example in St Sophia and in the Great Palace.[55] The influence of this can be seen in the use of the technique in the 'Arch of Chosroes' at Ctesiphon (sixth century A.D.), and the palace at Qasr ibn Warden in Syria.[56] The method is almost unknown in the West, but an instance does occur in a wall tower at Rome near the Porta Appia; it is possibly Honorian in date and is a brick groin vault built on a pitched brick principle.[57]

The use of fired brick in Greece and Asia Minor for major construction projects was presumably at first influenced by metropolitan use. However, the area was architecturally very fertile, and brick, cheap and versatile, was developed as a medium in its own right and became one of the main construction materials in the Eastern Mediterranean. The use and development of this material for wall construction and for vaulting in the two regions of Greece and Asia Minor looked forward to, and formed the basis for, the techniques of the Early Byzantine architects.

NOTES

[1] This paper is based on sections of the writer's doctoral thesis submitted in 1984 to the University of Newcastle upon Tyne, titled 'Building Materials and Techniques in the Eastern Mediterranean from the Hellenistic Period to the Fourth Century A.D.'. Professor R. M. Harrison and Mr J. C. Coulston read an earlier draft of this paper, for which I am very grateful. I should also like to thank Dr Susan Walker for access to information in her doctoral thesis.

[2] J. B. Ward-Perkins, *Roman Imperial Architecture* (Harmondsworth, 1981), 46–7.

[3] E. van Deman, 'Methods of determining the date of Roman concrete monuments', *AJA*, xvi (1912), 230–51, 387–432, esp. 413.

[4] An important study of brickwork in Roman Greece occurs in R. Ginouvès, *Le Theatron à gradins et l'odeion d'Argos* (Paris, 1972), 217–45.

[5] R. Koldeway, *The Excavations at Babylon* (London, 1912), 95.

[6] A. W. Lawrence, *Greek Architecture* (Harmondsworth, 1983), 318.

[7] R. F. Hoddinott, *Bulgaria in Antiquity* (London, 1975), 93–103.

[8] M. Colledge, *Parthian Art* (London, 1977), 26–7.

[9] J. B. Ward-Perkins, 'Notes on the structure and building methods of early Byzantine architecture', in D. Talbot-Rice (ed.), *The Great Palace of the Byzantine Emperors*, ii (Edinburgh, 1958), 86. An article is in preparation by the present writer on *opus reticulatum* in the Roman East which will deal with all known examples in the area.

[10] R. Traquair, 'Laconia: excavations at Sparta, 1906: the Roman stoa', *BSA*, iii (1905–6), 415–17.

[11] G. Hanfmann, *Sardis from Prehistoric to Roman Times* (Harvard, 1983), 59; personal observation.

[12] S. Walker, 'The Architectural Development of Roman Nymphaea in Greece', unpublished Ph.D. thesis, Institute of Archaeology, London, 1979, 209.

[13] A. J. B. Wace, 'Laconia: excavations at Sparta, 1906: the Roman baths', *BSA*, xii (1905–6), 407–17.

[14] I. F. Saunders, *Roman Crete* (Warminster, 1982), 57–88.

[15] M. Gough, 'Augusta Ciliciae', *AS*, vi (1956), 165–77.

[16] H. Dodge, 'The use of brick in Roman Asia Minor', *Yayla*, v (1984), 10; Dodge, *op. cit.* (note 1), 173, 241, 424.

[17] Ward-Perkins, *op. cit.* (note 9), 85.

[18] Ephesus: Harbour Baths, Theatre Baths; Tralles: Gymnasium (?); Aspendus: Aqueduct; Athens: Baths to south of Agora; Argos: Agora Baths, Aqueduct, Theatre Baths; Isthmia: Roman Baths; Cenchreae: Harbour Building; Olympia: Baths, Nymphaeum of Herodes Atticus.

[19] The whole subject of brick construction in the eastern provinces (Greece, Balkans, Asia Minor, Syria, etc.) is at present being prepared for detailed publication by the writer.

[20] Ward-Perkins, *op. cit.* (note 2), 233; for example the Barbarathermen, Trier.

[21] Ward-Perkins, *op. cit.* (note 2), 277.

[22] Ginouvès, *op. cit.* (note 4), 217–45.

[23] Hoddinott, *op. cit.* (note 7), 169, 244.

[24] Ankara: Ward-Perkins, *op. cit.* (note 2), 280; Aspendus: J. B. Ward-Perkins, 'The aqueduct at Aspendos', *PBSR*, xxiii (1955), 115–23; Nicaea: A. M. Schneider and W. Karnapp, *Die Stadtmauer von Iznik (Nicaea)*, Istanbuler Forschungen, ix (Berlin, 1938); personal observations.

[25] Thessalonica: Ward-Perkins, *op. cit.* (note 2), 449–54; O. Tafrali, *Topographie de Thessalonique* (Paris, 1913); Constantinople: B. Meyer-Plath and A. M. Schneider, *Die Landmauer von Konstantinopel*, ii (Berlin, 1943); Trier: D. Krenker and E. Krüger, *Die Trierer Kaiserthermen* (Augsburg, 1929); personal observations.

[26] J. G. Crow, 'Late Roman Fortifications in the Lower Danube Provinces: Aurelian to Anastasius', M.Litt. thesis, University of Newcastle upon Tyne, 1981, 60.

[27] This is situated to the north-west of the North Gate: personal observation. It is illustrated in J. Ch. Balty, *Guide d'Apamée* (Brussels, 1981), 172, pl. 187.

[28] C. Mango, *Byzantine Architecture* (New York, 1974), 146–51.

[29] F. W. Deichmann, 'Westliche Bautechnik in römischen und rhömaischen Osten', *RömMitt*, lxxxvi (1979), 447–527, esp. 526.

[30] Traquair, *op. cit.* (note 10), 415.

[31] Ginouvès, *op. cit.* (note 4), 226.

[32] Gough, *op. cit.* (note 15), 172–3.

[33] Ginouvès, *op. cit.* (note 4), 219 and 223.

[34] *Ibid.*, 226.

[35] *Ibid.*, 233; Ward-Perkins, *op. cit.* (note 9), 85.

[36] G. Lugli, *La tecnica edilizia romana* (Rome, 1957), 584–5.

[37] Traquair, *op. cit.* (note 10), 415; Wace, *op. cit.* (note 13), 407; Ginouvès, *op. cit.* (note 4), 224–7.

[38] R. Cagnat and V. Chapot, *Manuel d'archéologie romaine* (Paris, 1916), 25; Ginouvès, *op. cit.* (note 4), 217.

[39] Lugli, *op. cit.* (note 36), 583–630.

[40] The figures are those of van Deman, *op. cit.* (note 3); Lugli, *op. cit.* (note 36); Ward-Perkins, *op. cit.* (note 9); Ginouvès, *op. cit.* (note 4); Deichmann, *op. cit.* (note 29); and some recorded by the writer whilst in Turkey as an assistant on Professor R. M. Harrison's Lycian Survey.

[41] Ginouvès, *op. cit.* (note 4), 222.

[42] Van Deman, *op. cit.* (note 3), 413.

[43] Ginouvès, *op. cit.* (note 4), 233–4.

[44] The fact that brick-stamps do not occur may imply a different type of organization.

[45] Ward-Perkins, *op. cit.* (note 2), 251.

[46] J. B. Ward-Perkins, 'The architecture of Roman Anatolia: the Roman contribution', *Proceedings of the Xth International Congress of Classical Archaeology, Ankara, 1973* (Ankara, 1978), 881–91, esp. 888.

[47] Ward-Perkins, *op. cit.* (note 9), 88–95; Colledge, *op. cit.* (note 8), 26.

[48] The origins of pitched brick vaulting and the early, as well as the Roman, examples are discussed in Dodge, *op. cit.* (note 1), 242–7.

[49] M. I. Rostovtzeff, *The Excavations at Dura-Europos: Preliminary Report of the Sixth Season of Work, 1932–33* (New Haven, 1936), 66, 86, 93.

[50] A. E. R. Boak and E. E. Petersen, *Karanis: Topographical and Architectural Report of Excavations 1924–28* (Ann Arbor, 1931), 23; A. E. R. Boak, *Soknopaiou Nesos* (Ann Arbor, 1935), 12.

[51] Argos: Walker, *op. cit.* (note 12), 163; A. Choisy, *L'Art de bâtir chez les Romains* (Paris, 1873), 173, fig. 173.

[52] These are not mentioned in the publication by R. Naumann and S. Kantar, 'Die Agora von Smyrna', *Istanbuler Forschungen*, xvii (1950), 69–114.

[53] Aspendus: Ward-Perkins, *op. cit.* (note 9), 96; Rhodiapolis: C. Bayburtuoğlu, *Lycie* (n.d.), pl. between 16 and 17.

[54] Ward-Perkins, *op. cit.* (note 2), 453; H. J. Cowan, *The Masterbuilders* (London, 1979), 65; personal observation.

[55] Ward-Perkins, *op. cit.* (note 9), 59; R. Krautheimer, *Early Christian and Byzantine Architecture* (London, 1979), 219.

[56] Ward-Perkins, *op. cit.* (note 9), 95; Colledge, *op. cit.* (note 8), 64; Mango, *op. cit.* (note 28), 146–51.

[57] I am grateful to Mr J. C. Coulston of the Department of Archaeology, University of Newcastle upon Tyne, for this information.

Index

Compiled by Carmen O. Lange

117